RUDE
awakenings

RUDE

awakenings

Overcoming the Civility Crisis in the Workplace

GIOVINELLA GONTHIER

with Kevin Morrissey

Dearborn™
Trade Publishing
A **Kaplan Professional** Company

This publication is designed to provide accurate and authoritative information in regard to the subject matter covered. It is sold with the understanding that the publisher is not engaged in rendering legal, accounting, or other professional service. If legal advice or other expert assistance is required, the services of a competent professional person should be sought.

Senior Acquisitions Editor: Jean Iversen
Senior Managing Editor: Jack Kiburz
Interior Design: Lucy Jenkins
Cover Design: Jody Billert, Billert Communications
Typesetting: Elizabeth Pitts

Published by Dearborn Trade Publishing, a Kaplan Professional Company

Printed in the United States of America

02 03 04 10 9 8 7 6 5 4 3 2 1

Library of Congress Cataloging-in-Publication Data

Gonthier, Giovinella.
  Rude awakenings : overcoming the civility crisis in the workplace / By Giovinella Gonthier with Kevin Morrissey.
      p. cm.
Includes index.
  ISBN 0-7931-5197-X
  1. Employee morale. 2. Employee competitive behavior. 3. Courtesy in the workplace. I. Title: Civility crisis in the workplace. II. Morrissey, Kevin. III. Title.
  HF5549.5.M6 G658   2002
  658.3'145 – dc21

                                        2001008237

Dedication

To my father, Wilbur D. Gonthier, and to my husband, Roger G. Wilson—both exemplars of civility

ACKNOWLEDGMENTS

To all the organizations and their employees who provided me with material for the book, especially Boeing, SAS, Shell, Sprint, and Southwest Airlines. Your trust, graciously lent time, and willingness to share knowledge and resources for the benefit of others are truly remarkable. (Your graciousness stands out all the more because not all companies treated me so respectfully or agreed to help.) You have enhanced the quality of this book beyond measure and I thank you for believing in civility.

To the brave souls who have endorsed my book and recognize that civility is a "nice and necessary" core value for any successful organization.

To Nancy Norton, my former history professor at Wheaton College in Massachusetts, for reading my first chapter and ensuring my historical chronological accuracy. And to all the teachers I have had in my life, worldwide, for your encouragement and perseverance. You get short shrift and poor pay but still work hard to shape us.

To Ed Johnson, the current president of the Chicago chapter of the American Society for Training and Development, for seeing civility as an emerging issue and championing my work as a practitioner.

To Iva Pavicic for adding to my knowledge of organizational development.

To Ann and Duane Carlson for their keen interest in the project, advice, good dinners, and help with the quiz at the end of the book.

To Nancy Angelopoulos, Beth Lisberg, and Patricia Simms for their technological skill in preparing my original hand-drawn diagrams for the computer.

To Jean Iversen, my editor at Dearborn, for sensing the civility crisis out there, deciding to do something creative about it, and allowing me to present a book about respect that is different from the thousands of business etiquette books in print.

Finally, to my friend, Kevin Morrissey, for finessing my text. I have just realized that we worked through this project from start to end without a contract—and are not only still talking but still good friends! This is a true mark of civility and of a substantial friendship of more than a quarter of a century. Your gift of making this manuscript more compelling is just another dimension of your substance. I am fortunate to have had your backing for so long. Thank you.

!@!%#!@!%#!@!%#!@!%#!@!%#!@!%#!@!%#!@!%#!@!%#!@!%#!@!

CONTENTS

INTRODUCTION

If we are to overcome rampant incivility in the workplace, we must first define what we mean by civility. More than a half-century ago—long before we faced a crisis of current proportions—the eminent British sociologist Edward Shils proposed such characteristics as courtesy, moderation, respect for others, and self-restraint, saying that in all of these "there are intimations of considerations for the sensibilities of other people and particularly for their desire to be esteemed."

Civility, or respect as it is sometimes called, can be interpreted in many different ways in today's highly compartmentalized society. Many first think of etiquette and mastering certain social rituals. When we look at civility specifically in the workplace setting, some of us conjure up having more physical space and better working conditions, some link it to diversity and the equal treatment of everyone, and others view it solely as avoiding sexual harassment. We may not even equate incivility with our own "snippy" or inconsiderate behavior.

Having lived and worked all over the world and encountered all kinds of rudeness, bullying, maltreatment, and injustice, I take a broad view of civility: Civility is being mindful of the dignity of the human being in your sphere at all times. Civility is not so much about niceties as it is about the way we live our lives overall and the way we treat other people. It is not patterned behavior but something much more essential that emanates from within.

I became aware of the civility crisis while pursuing a protocol business and discovering the increasingly insensitive and inconsiderate manner in which visiting dignitaries were treated in most business settings. I was just as shocked about workers' behavior toward each other and about their slovenly attire, even as they milled in lobbies elegantly decorated with art and fresh flowers. Materialism was paramount—but not interpersonal behavior.

As I began to grasp the full extent of the problem, I saw management and human resources personnel in every sector of our economy—private industry, government, academia, or not-for-profit—grappling with widespread bad behavior in the workplace. Looking deeper, I realized the negative implications for both the bottom line and the wellness of the organizations and individuals who worked for them.

These business leaders are searching for solutions with an urgency I would have to call desperate. This book is a response to that desperation. *Rude Awakenings: Overcoming the Civility Crisis in the Workplace* shows how to identify incivility, cultivate behaviors with which to replace it, and build and maintain a culture of civility in the workplace. It starts with looking at how and why incivility has evolved to its modern-day dimensions, and leads to raising awareness of the incivility that now permeates the workplace, regardless of job or rank, and to looking at our own behavioral patterns before criticizing others for their bad behavior. After all, it is usually the incivility of our superiors, colleagues, or customers that we recognize—seldom our own!

My approach, unlike that embodied by traditional business etiquette books, is to focus on specific, problematic issues in the workplace and to teach replacement strategies that are more conducive to productivity and personal well-being. Readers are encouraged to take ownership of their bad behaviors, unlearn them, and replace them with the more constructive behaviors suggested in actual work-related scenarios. I constantly challenge them to see themselves and their coworkers in these situations and offer remedies they can envision in their own work settings. In providing real workday scenarios, I have tried to be realistic and use the actual, if at times vulgar, language that is common to the workplace. My purpose is not so much dramatic effect as authenticity.

I go on to provide competency tools in the form of modules for teaching a civility course and discuss in detail how to conduct an organizational campaign to implement a civility program.

Rude Awakenings: Overcoming the Civility Crisis in the Workplace offers a compelling look at bad behavior on the job in our times. Incivilities in the modern workplace run the gamut from the annoying to the violent. There is very public in-your-face incivility, such as yelling and fist pounding, and more subtle and covert varieties, such as chipping away at someone's self-esteem through constant slights or by refusing to permit sufficient bereavement time for an employee who has suffered a loss.

Power variables in the workplace hierarchy can come into play, and the complex dynamics are not always clear. Some people in authority abuse their power and browbeat employees, but incivility is not always downward. There is horizontal incivility between colleagues, and upward incivility can occur when an abusive subordinate spots weakness in a supervisor. There is in-character bad behavior, that of the person who is frequently uncivil, rude, and mean-spirited, as well as inadvertent incivility, which can be caused by a situation or even a hormonal imbalance. I treat most of these distinctions generically when examining specific workplace issues and strategies. In any event, the problem needs to be resolved, and preventing escalation depends on the conflict management skills of the individuals directly involved or those brought in to intervene. I have tried to encompass all types of generic incivility, with an eye toward interventions that prevent escalation.

In the language of incivility, an instigator is the person who initiates an uncivil episode, while the target bears the brunt of the tirade. (Bear in mind that at times, although rare, it may be unclear who is in which role!) Bullying is incivility that is persistent and that inflicts emotional distress and pain on the target. It is a serious and growing workplace problem that has recently been addressed in the legal codes of some European countries, but which often receives short shrift in the United States, where it is still not illegal. In the United States, a bully may be referred to as a jerk.

I am well aware of the impact of culture on behavior and have addressed it in the realm of global business. While realizing that we live in an increasingly heterogeneous society, I do not believe that our diversity needs to be a cause of incivility in the workplace. All cultures have a normative benchmark of what is considered acceptable behavior, accompanied by ritualistic manners and respect for authority. If managers effectively set a level of expectation, they will overcome such problems as people from different cultures viewing time commitments differently.

In closing, I cannot overemphasize that the time to act is now! We can no longer afford the ill effects of incivility on our communities or our economies. Focusing for a moment on the United States, where the problem is particularly severe, let us heed the words of President George W. Bush in his inaugural address in January 2001, in which he surveyed the tenor and the needs of the times. Specifically invoking civility several times in his address, President Bush commented: "We must live up to the calling we share. Civility is not a tactic or a sentiment. It is the determined choice of trust over cynicism, of community over chaos. And this commitment, if we keep it, is a way to shared accomplishment."

CHAPTER 1

The Evolution of Incivility in Our Times

You get into your car on a dark, cold, blustery winter morning for the long commute to work. To make the hour's drive more tolerable, you turn on the CD player expecting to hear some soothing classical music. Instead, you are rudely awakened by a rap CD your teenage daughter left in the player the night before. Vulgar themes and language are hard to take at any time, but especially so early in the morning. You turn it off and choose to listen to the radio, but the blasting airwaves are full of shock jocks whose adoring fans phone in all kinds of rude and lewd comments from their cellular phones. Silence is indeed going to be golden for you today! You navigate through the bumper-to-bumper traffic, preoccupied with thoughts of the deteriorating quality of life and what awaits you at work that day. Suddenly, someone in an expensive car cuts you off without warning—no turn signal, no nod or gesture requesting permission to be let in, nothing. While your foot hits the brake to avoid an accident and you sound the horn in warning, he flips you the bird as though the near mishap were your fault.

No wonder you arrive at the office irritable and impatient. Many of your colleagues began their workdays with similarly harrowing commutes and are in equally upset states. All it will take

1

to ignite a conflict is an ignored voice mail or e-mail, a thought-less comment, or a perceived slight.

The same conditions that cause rudeness in our society at large lead to incivility in the workplace—an air of entitlement given off by some, a sense of alienation afflicting others, the trap of relentless technological connection, the stress of overcrowd-ing and overwork, failure to understand burgeoning diversity, and rapidly changing expectations for which we have been ill-prepared.

Stir into the pot the erosion of many long-standing values and the dwindling influence of family and traditional institutions in shaping and instilling replacement behaviors, and you have a foolproof recipe for incivility.

Our current civility crisis is caused by converging factors, none of which can be addressed alone. In the web that these de-velopments have spun, societal forces are all tugging and pulling at each other. It's not a pretty picture, as our harried commuter in the previous example and the masses of likewise beleaguered U.S. American workers can attest. So just how did we arrive at this pla-teau of bad behavior, lack of consideration, and obliviousness to the needs and feelings of our fellow human travelers? Let's take a closer look at the root causes of modern-day incivility.

Affluenza: The Dark Side of Unprecedented Success

Coined in the 1950s to describe the energetic economic growth spawned by a U.S. workforce tired of wartime rations and restrictions, the term *affluenza* has since become synony-mous with the latter 20th-century epidemic of overwork, stress, and indebtedness that has struck so many who relentlessly chase the good life.

It is characterized by an addiction to consumption, a need to make more and more money to fuel the relentless pursuit of the American dream, and a belief that one's worth is intrinsically tied to one's income bracket. If you suffer from affluenza, you work excessively to acquire an array of things that you don't really need. You are stuck on a "work and spend" treadmill with little time to enjoy much of anything else in your life. You're saddled with debts and the resulting stress, and afraid of losing the job that provides you the paycheck to buy all the stuff.

The optimism of a victorious U.S. American public after World War II generated a creative vitality that led to enormous and unprecedented wealth. Credit cards were introduced into the mainstream economy soon after, with "charge it" destined to become one of the most common phrases in the English language.

Thus began the culture of acquisition that has been spiraling out of hand ever since and that was the subject of a 2000 PBS network documentary also called *Affluenza.* The marketplace has come to exert an enormous power over our lives, manipulating us to think in certain ways and to consume on demand. Advertising has become frighteningly adept at promoting consumer goods and making us yearn for more. Not many of us think in spiritual terms anymore—we are too consumed by material concerns and the need to keep up. No one would think of sharing the trappings of everyday life with friends or neighbors; we must own everything outright.

Affluenza ebbed a little in the 1970s with the oil shortage, high interest rates, and inflation, but it came back strong in the 1980s. In *Wall Street,* the Academy Award–winning movie of 1987, the ruthlessly driven financier Gordon Gekko's exclamation "Greed is good!" defined the ambitions of the decade. Gekko exemplified the impetuous, rude, "everyone else be damned" personality that many had come to consider a territorial imperative of wealth by the close of the century, when the soaring wealth of the dot-com generation raised the standard for arrogance, selfishness, conspicuous consumption, and waste.

Because success is almost always equated with money rather than with achievement in our culture, we have to a large extent empowered people with money to be nasty. We make excuses for their bad behavior, rationalizing "but he or she is successful." Money creates an attitude of entitlement and impulsiveness, with no thought about the consequences—whatever I want (never mind if I need it), I will get. That attitude carries over into all facets of life and encourages a loss of self-restraint. If I am rich and I feel like saying "f--k" in a conversation, I do. If I have the urge to kick, scream, demand, condescend, or otherwise behave outrageously in public, I will.

Take, for example, the U.S. American banker, traveling on business from Buenos Aires to New York in first class on United Airlines flight #976 in October of 1995 en route to his home in Connecticut. After being refused more alcohol because of his drunken state and loud, abusive language, he climbed on top of a beverage cart and defecated, proceeding to track feces through the first-class cabin on linen napkins!

If you think this was an isolated incident I dredged up to make a sensational point, think again. These days, most people could tell some pretty amazing true tales of the incivility they have encountered in public places where such behavior would have been unthinkable just a few years ago.

It used to be that people with wealth and position felt compelled to be role models of civility and gentility, especially in business and civic settings. If you had money, you were expected to behave with a certain decorum. Your children were sent to finishing school or received private tutorials in etiquette; you were concerned about them behaving properly and being accepted by others. Nowadays, the doormen and valets in our luxury highrises often are more polite, better spoken, and better dressed than the residents they serve. They have an incentive to be civil, while their well-off patrons no longer do!

The Legacy of the 1960s:
Casual Becomes Chaotic

As a prospering U.S. American public began to enjoy the mobility provided by money during the postwar years, people started to feel the stirrings of more freedom in other aspects of their lives as well. The generation of young people coming of age in the 1960s felt stifled by societal boundaries, many of which were arbitrary, racist, and sexist.

During these turbulent years, they set into motion far-reaching change that profoundly altered our society for the better. Women were no longer confined to their husbands' shadows, nor African-Americans to separate accommodations; Native Americans were no longer kept on reservations, nor Jews out of clubs. This generation valued inclusion and built the foundation for reforms still to come, such as respecting gays and lesbians and protecting the rights of the disabled. Certainly, my concept of civility—being mindful of the dignity of the human being in your sphere—developed out of the struggles of that era. Although I was too young to be involved and had not yet immigrated to the United States, the nobility of these changes affected me profoundly.

However, discarding what was rotten and uncivil in U.S. American society, the 1960s generation threw out everything— the good along with the bad, the proverbial baby with the bathwater. As protest focused increasingly on an unpopular war, young people became disillusioned with a government caught up in lies and they lost respect for tradition. All forms of deference and respect soon disappeared.

When this generation reared their own children, it was with a great deal more permissiveness. These new parents were still angry about the constraints of the old rules and too busy trying to create a world characterized by extolling basic human rights and peace to worry about formulating new social rituals more in line with their values. The result was that the generation that followed grew up without ever learning much about the rudiments of manners and civility.

As the cycle continued, some things began to revert. Now that civil rights was a given and there was no military draft to object to, making money once again became important, only now in a milieu without the trappings of civility. No doubt, ensuing generations developed their own norms of respect. Generation X rediscovered concern about the environment and became more sensitive to remarks that might sound sexist. But the new norms do not necessarily make up for old norms that are disappearing. While you may be more sensitive toward women, you may still talk loudly on your cellular phone in a public place. While you may respect the environment, you may still leave your trash all around the break room, expecting others to pick up after you.

We have become a disposable culture—we routinely discard what is handed down by previous generations in our search for personal relevance. This supposedly promotes creativity and ingenuity in a high-tech world. But any student of history knows that intelligent people learn from the mistakes and successes of those who preceded them. You have to constantly sift through cultural heritage, redefining some aspects as needed but retaining what works.

Returning to the generation that rewove the social fabric in the 1960s, we find them now in control of the workplace and ever the leaders in changing tradition. Once in the vanguard of counterculture dress—dashiki shirts, frayed jeans, and tie-dyed garments—they quickly proceeded to phase out suits and ties once they set the rules. After all, we no longer wore uniforms to school, dressed up to go to worship, or entertained formally. Casual dress in the workplace soon became the trend of the day, hyped to foster innovation and more open communication.

No one, however, thought through just how the more informal corporate climate fostered by casual dress would affect employee self-perceptions and coworker interactions. Over time it became clear that casual dress led to a casual mentality. If I am dressed, the reasoning seems to go, I can let down my guard. And when that happens, everything becomes more relaxed—speech, written grammar, posture, and body language. Casual dress bred familiarity and undermined standards of interactional behavior in the business setting.

Other problems with the well-intentioned move to casual dressing were the lack of forethought about its potential abuse and little in the way of specifications defining what constituted casual dress. If you dispensed with the tie and the coat, did you still have to iron your shirt and your pants? Or bathe before you put them on? (This sounds extreme, but lack of personal hygiene has become a serious workplace problem.) Did casual dressing mean that you could wear spaghetti straps that allowed your bra straps to show, or shorts with holes in them? When power dressing was popular a decade earlier, it was widely written about and the subject of training seminars. But when it came to casual dressing, everyone was left to his or her own devices.

The importance of defining expectations and making them well known to employees during any period of change in corporate culture cannot be overemphasized. With the onset of casual dressing, the majority of companies did little to prepare employees. In most cases, no expectations were spelled out and no campaign was instituted to further understanding of the objective. It was just assumed that everyone would know what was meant and would dress accordingly. Employees were not told that shorts, sneakers, bare midriffs, and see-through clothing were unacceptable, so when people showed up inappropriately dressed in this manner and were criticized, it led to shouting matches, ill will, and workplace tension.

Now, it is generally accepted that dressing up has a ripple effect on other aspects of our behavior—we behave in a more decorous and businesslike manner. When the workplace went casual, the lines between what is and is not appropriate professional behavior became blurred. Many people became confused and ultimately concluded that anything goes.

Diversity: Equality and the Demise of Common Courtesy

The changing roles of minorities and women in World War II and their impact on sustaining the U.S. war effort and economy launched a permanent transformation in the makeup of American society. Up to that point, African-Americans and women had been largely left out of mainstream corporate society and restricted from entering certain businesses.

By the 1960s, thanks to the forces of reform operating in the society at large and the civil rights movement and the women's movement in particular, the multicultural nature of the population began at long last to be reflected in mainstream businesses. Equal opportunity was law. The daughters of those women who returned to the home after World War II were now going to work en masse. Not far behind was the Native American reawakening, gays and lesbians coming out of the closet to demand their human rights, and the disabled organizing to fight for access and dignity.

The workforce was changing dramatically, not only in terms of makeup but also in terms of empowerment. Add to that the influx of African, Arab, Asian, Caribbean, and Latino immigrants during the 1970s through the 1990s and the U.S. American sociological tapestry resembled a more finished work.

However, a funny thing happened on the way to becoming a more just society. As we more firmly embraced the precept that people are equal, many of the manners and rituals of behavior that had existed through a period of inequality lost their meaning. You may say "Good morning, Miss Annie" to your housekeeper and give her two dollars for doing your laundry. But as soon as she tells you she has a better opportunity elsewhere and is no longer going to be your laundress, you stop greeting her or recognizing her existence and worth. Or take the case of deference based on gender. Men used to gladly give up their seats on buses to women when women were not viewed as equal; now that women have demanded equality, men won't give up their seats even if women are eight months pregnant!

Certainly, some of the rudeness toward women can be traced back to the 1970s, when the superfeminists rejected all kinds of manners as a sign of weakness and told off men who opened doors for them. But the roots of modern-day incivility run deeper than just reaction. Equality now seems to serve as an excuse to stop being polite and helpful to one another. It is as though in obtaining equality we laid the groundwork for doing away with common courtesy. In fact, the phrase "common courtesy" may be considered an oxymoron in the 21st century because courtesy is no longer common. Rudeness is one of the few bad behaviors still permissible—it has not been legislated, mandated, or peer-pressured out of existence. So maybe people behave badly just because they can!

Some folks are rude because they're angry about losing the prestige or standing they once had. They resent the reality of equality and will punish you for it by behaving disrespectfully toward you. "You are now my equal, so screw you" is the rationale. Yet these days the incivility is just as likely to stem from the formerly oppressed as from the former oppressor. If I ask someone in a wheelchair in the supermarket parking lot if she needs help loading grocery bags into her car, does she have to look at me and say "No!" with such contempt? Can't she simply say, "Thanks, but I can manage."

Too many people associate good manners with the unequal relationships they were often used to prop up, with one person having power over another. When these roles changed, we failed to see that courtesy is really just a question of one person being kind to another, that good behavior, in fact, eases our stresses and improves our lives. As we became a more equal society, we forgot that civility can celebrate equality and that there are diverse ways to show civility.

Much has been written about diversity contributing to rudeness, postulating that because we are now so diverse, the only thing we have in common is the lowest common denominator. I disagree with this assessment. Being blessed with different cultures and characteristics does not mean that we cannot all aspire to civility. We no longer have neither a white Protestant majority culture nor a singular "American" way of doing things.

Some of us now come to work with our hair braided with beads. Why should everyone have to have straight hair, when we are not all born with straight hair? Some of us remove our hats when we enter the workplace, while others come from a culture in which turbans or other head coverings commonly are worn inside all day long. None of these differences precludes us from being polite and well behaved—"Thank you" in any language conveys the same sentiment.

The bottom line is that incivility should be considered just as inexcusable and unacceptable as racism and harassment, because civility enables us to build a fairer society.

Urban Overcrowding:
We're Stressed Out before We Even Start

The growing population and the increasing population density in our cities has only exacerbated the diversity debate. Too little space causes tensions—especially if you have to share that space with people you do not want to understand!

According to the U.S. Census 2000 report, the population in the United States increased by 32.7 million between 1990 and 2000. This was the largest ten-year increase in U.S. history and the first time in the 20th century that all states showed population gains, especially in large urban centers. However, population density is the real irritant and breeding ground for incivility. In 2000, more than eight out of ten people in the nation (a whopping 226 million) lived in metropolitan areas.

Once derelict inner-city areas are rapidly being rezoned and rebuilt with luxury housing, a phenomenon the sociologists call reurbanization. Living further from work doesn't necessarily help with the density problem either, for many of the suburbs are suffering from the same overbuilding mentality and congestion; these once sleepy bedroom communities have become bustling towns with smaller-scale versions of the same problems that plague urban centers. Even the farmlands surrounding our cities, once refuges of open space, are being turned into subdevelopments at alarming rates.

During the 1950s, the decade that had previously shown the greatest growth, urban planners designed new communities with broad boulevards and parks. Houses and apartment buildings were spaced to allow for sunlight. These days, city politicians looking for a dense power and revenue base find urban developers only too willing to collaborate in the proliferation of sardine-can highrises and subdivisions. Never mind that one building blocks out the sunlight from the other. Never mind that developers are permitted even to build over railroad tracks and on sandy slivers of river shores. Never mind that we have significantly less room in which to work, play, live, and park—the consequence of which inevitably is rage.

Other countries plan new cities from scratch to help alleviate congestion and accommodate growing populations. This solution has not entered our national psyche as yet; and if it does, the endless debates, studies, and wrangling for control will take a half-century to implement. Sadly, the justification at the neighborhood planning level for sardine-can development is usually an anticipated increase in property values. Once the neighborhood that we moved into because there was a little open space becomes more congested, it is inevitably argued, we can sell our homes at a premium and move somewhere else—as though making money and moving on was the only value in life.

One of the ironies of all this development is that the revenue raised is not bringing wider roads with more lanes to accommodate the extra traffic that it generates, or more rail tracks, trains, or buses for better mass transportation. There is less room to maneuver around in, and this increases our sense of helplessness and feelings of losing control over our lives. If you have been cut off deliberately on the expressway—like the harried commuter cited as an example at the start of this chapter—and it takes you an extra 45 minutes to get to work, you are likely to arrive in a rage, but you know that only too well!

The 2001 Urban Mobility Study, released by Texas A&M University's Texas Transportation Institute, found that the percentage of freeway lanes that were congested grew from about 35 percent in 1982 to 65 percent by 1999. The study also determined that during rush hour, it takes 40 percent longer to make a typical trip; in 1982, that same trip took only 16 percent longer during rush hour than at off-peak times. When you spend 40 percent more of your morning commute in backups, this takes a toll on the workday. And there is no end in sight, for our growing affluence is only adding to the congestion—now that we have multiple cars and every member of the family can be driving on the highway at the same time!

!@!%#!@!%#!@!%#!@!%#!@!%#!@!%#!@!%#!@!%#!@!%#!@!%#!@!

Ten Reasons Why We Behave Uncivilly

1. We're working ourselves ragged just so we can buy too many things we really don't need.

2. We often put up with outrageously bad behavior by financially successful people and then feel compelled to make excuses for them.

3. Many of the people we work with every day were raised with little training about manners.

4. When our employers tried such experiments as "casual dress," they failed to formulate guidelines or think through the effects.

5. Too many people see common courtesy as behavior that perpetuates inequality, failing to see that civility is simply being kind to one another.

6. Our urban communities are inhumanely dense and our commutes to work often horrific.

7. Young people today enter the work world from families and schools that increasingly fail to set and enforce rules and limits about behavior.

8. A frightening number of our neighbors are feeling so alienated, isolated, and anonymous that they can be rude with no remorse or fear of reciprocation.

9. There's little fairness and loyalty left in today's highly transient workplace.

10. Rather than improve our work lives, technology has stripped us of support services, dehumanized the workplace, and plugged us in around the clock.

Decline in Family Life and Community:
We're on Our Own

Just when we most need support systems to cope with over-work, overcrowding, and all kinds of other stresses, the crumbling house of cards that is modern life is taking its toll on our own families. Traditional households are in decline and have lost much of their influence as rule-setting structures. New familial structures, including gay and lesbian couples who adopt and single parents with strong support systems and the stamina to do the work of two parents, are picking up some of the slack. Nonetheless, the sociologists tell us that there is turmoil and dysfunction in today's families.

In 1950, only 22 percent of householders were unmarried; by 2000, that number had risen to 48 percent. (This also means more homes, more developments, less space, and more congestion!) The number of families headed by single mothers has increased 25 percent just since 1990. Contributing to these numbers is a high rate of divorce—almost 50 percent—and out-of-wedlock births. Through most of the 1990s, a little more than a third of all the babies in the United States were born to unmarried women. (Although high, this figure is lower than those in the United Kingdom, France, and Scandinavia.) Furthermore, marriage rates are dropping throughout the industrialized world.

Fewer and fewer children are currently raised by two parents (not that all two-parent families are doing such a great job raising children at the start of the new millennium). The time pressure alone on single-parent households, however, is enormous—there is simply less time to spend with the children teaching them values. Every statistical measure I have seen suggests that children raised by single parents do less well than their playmates from two-parent households.

With less parental supervision, children have more opportunity to watch TV, chat on the phone or at the computer, and hang out at the mall. The quality of our children's entertainment leaves much to be desired. Films and television are crass wastelands, and much of our popular music is vulgar. The message disseminated is not only that all of this lewdness is acceptable, but that the values embodied are worth imitating.

No matter what the configuration of the family, we have, in general, become a harried society striving to keep up with the Joneses in the acquisition game (see the previous discussion of affluenza). Economic pressure to buy costly 21st-century "toys" is limiting our role in our children's moral and character development. They come home from school to an empty house because we're still on the treadmill. We feel guilty about being absent from their lives, so we fail to punish bad behavior and try to make up for our absence by buying them more material "stuff," but children who do not have a sense of belonging, of being part of a greater whole, grow up isolated and do not feel part of a community.

Most parents teach their children that they are special—that their self-esteem is important, but often in these times they forget to teach that other people are special, too, that the feelings of others are also significant. The message that relationships are about reciprocity and not just feeling good about one's self is not always passed on. So without respect for others being taught in the home, children go into the world—and subsequently into the workforce—without a good grounding in civility.

By absence and omission, today's parents are only doing what most other traditionally influential bodies, from educators to workplace leaders, have been doing in recent decades—abdicating their roles as rule makers and enforcers. Our major religions still teach the Golden Rule, but they preach to a shrinking and increasingly autonomous following, with fewer children receiving religious instruction. Everyone else is afraid of setting expectations and no one wants to promulgate rules. The current milieu is one of "suspending judgment," which has unfortunately also resulted in suspending common sense.

We do not make the time to teach about responsibility in its three forms—social, professional, and personal. If children do not grow up learning about respect, how can we expect people in the work world to know about it? Parents abdicate teaching civility to the schools. The schools see this as a "soft" skill and therefore less important to teach than technology, which is more quantifiable and might help garner additional funding. And let's face it, a computer course is macho and machines make neat sounds, unlike the namby-pamby stuff of civility.

Instead of being role models, parents are often the exemplars of rudeness. Take, for example, the jeering, booing, and foul language increasingly directed at coaches and other children by parents attending junior league sporting events. The problem has become so severe that a summit had to be held by one officiating organization to find solutions to these angry and sometimes critical outbursts. *One of the findings was that parents and fans had never been told that such conduct was not permissible.*

You might think I'm exaggerating and ask how this could possibly be, but as a trainer in civility, I'm not surprised. I've found that when you are brought up in a culture without boundaries, and whose economic system encourages impulsiveness, anything is permissible. You have a house and a car that are bigger than your parents had—in our culture, that means that you can throw your weight around! No one is going to object. When people and institutions are afraid to make rules and correct others for bad behavior, when judgment is suspended, people are honestly not aware about what is permissible and what is not.

We live in a society without limits. No one is setting or enforcing acceptable standards of behavior, and everyone is pointing a finger at everyone else for this failure. To return briefly to the simple but shocking example of parents not knowing how to behave at their children's sports events, when our children learn from us that bad behavior on the playing field is preferable to shaking hands before a game and congratulating the winners afterward, they carry that baggage to the workplace later on in life. I think the applicable phrase here is "Monkey see, monkey do!"

Coming from homes that are awash in dysfunction gives us a sense of being alone on the planet. We grow up without strong bonds to anyone or anything. We have become anonymous. And when you feel anonymous, without a sense of belonging, you can give the finger on the highway and not feel remorseful. When you arrive late for work in your transient, high-density community, you can fight and cuss for that parking space without batting an eyelid, because you neither know nor care about the other person who also wants to park there.

Have you ever wondered why folks in small towns, which tend to have more permanent and stable populations, are so much nicer to each other? When you know the people you come into contact with on your daily rounds, you can't afford to lose your temper because sooner or later you will have to face them again. If, on the other hand, there is little sense of community, everything becomes me, me, me. People are not in a sharing mode but are in a survival mode. We can easily make a vulgar gesture to someone and then go hide behind voice mail and e-mail.

As I wrote this chapter, my computer was hit by a virus that penetrated my hard drive and randomly sent out files—including unpublished data—not only to people in my address book, but also to strangers. This type of cybersabotage is a nightmare for all concerned! However, it got me thinking about people who write computer viruses and how they fit into our discussion on incivility.

I have read that no one seems to know exactly why people create computer viruses, but a sociologist friend of mine attributes it to alienation from society, rejection, and loneliness. If you sit in your basement feeling isolated, angry, and anonymous, it does not matter if you create a vicious virus intended to harm a stranger. You probably feel entitled to impose your destructive knowledge on others you do not know or respect.

Sleep Deprivation: We're Too Tired to Cope

Sleep deprivation has become such an issue in the modern United States that it cannot be left out of any discussion of stressors that cause incivility in the workplace. According to the

National Sleep Foundation's 2001 Sleep in America Poll, fully 63 percent of U.S. American adults do not get the amount of sleep recommended for good health, safety, and optimum work performance.

Compared to five years ago, almost as many adults say they now spend more time at work as say they spend less time sleeping. More than 38 percent say they are working 50 hours or more a week. (Remember, we have to keep up with the Joneses and acquire stuff!) This reallocation of time and the prioritization of work have a direct effect on sleep—those who work more, sleep less. The same study found that one in five adults is so sleepy during the day that it interferes with daily activities.

My friends overseas always tell me how lucky we are in this country, where many cities never go to sleep. We can run errands at night, because many businesses are open 24 hours a day to accommodate those who work long hours, extra jobs, and night shifts. But this can encourage unhealthy and sometimes antisocial lifestyles. The often exploited workers of the 19th century worked long, hard hours, but they were able to get away from their work at night. When they were home, they were able to rest. Now we're plugged in, online, and on call most of the day and night.

According to a June 2001 report by MSN Health and WebMD, insomnia in the United States costs approximately $100 billion a year in medical costs and decreased productivity. According to the report, even modest alterations in waking and sleeping habits can lead to anxiety, stress, and depression. No wonder people come to work in a snappy and irritable frame of mind!

The Brave New Work World: Transient and Technologically Driven

Once upon a time, U.S. Americans labored in stable work environments where they could stay for most of their career. It wasn't all that long ago that the average worker changed jobs about as many times in a lifetime as we now do in a few years. The workplace has become highly transient, and this has profoundly affected our values.

We no longer care as much about fairness, loyalty, or goodwill. In boom times when employment is high, people feel that they can always change jobs if they are not happy. More job choices and greater mobility lessen bonds and encourage lax behavior in an atmosphere seen as temporary. This hardly encourages cohesiveness.

In slow economic times with downsizing and budget cuts, many temporary workers are hired both in the professional realm and in administrative areas. These workers are not seen as colleagues and are often treated with disdain by permanent employees. The temps, who in turn know that their tenure may be short, often do not bother to build good relationships. I hear over and over again in my workshops that very few temps are sent out into the workforce with civility training of any type and that their behavior frequently borders on the obnoxious.

Disrespectful and demeaning treatment of workers nurtures a climate of indifference and disloyalty. Another major contributing factor to our current climate of incivility was the callous downsizing of the 1980s, when corporations laid off longtime employees without much concern for health care insurance, pensions, or other significant factors affecting their future wellbeing. I know of people who were given an hour to clear their desks and then escorted out the front door by security personnel (as though they were criminals), even though they had worked at a company for 15 years. No dignity, no decorum.

Many of the outplacement firms that sprang up during those times prevented this conduct from happening again, but previously laid-off employees have long memories. When they go to other jobs, they may worry that they can be fired and escorted out without respect all over again. If the employer is not going to value loyalty and dedication, why bother?

The reengineering of corporate work structures during the late 1980s and 1990s also heightened incivility. Hierarchical structures were flattened into teams and matrix organizations without the benefit of civility training and little thought about how to handle resulting interpersonal problems. The leader of a new team may be an executive assistant, for example, to whom an executive vice president on the team doesn't know how to react.

In theory, the new group leaders are to coach members to reach consensus; but if we are being coached by someone younger who has a different vocabulary and little sense of respect for others, the purpose begins to fall apart. I have also witnessed leaders who are so busy that coaching becomes little other than barking orders, and the team quickly becomes dysfunctional. For a team to work well, its members must possess good interpersonal skills.

But the same companies that spend millions of dollars on technology training don't place a priority on teaching people skills, so the people go and hide behind their machines. One of the major training problems in the 1980s and 1990s was that Human Resources and Training departments put all their efforts into high-tech training and neglected the so-called "soft" skills, such as manners and civility. Now we have a whole generation of employees skilled in computers who lack basic people skills.

Technology presents its own set of frustrations. Software becomes obsolete fast and must be upgraded. After learning one system the past year, you may have to take time out of your busy schedule to take another course to learn another system this year. Participants in my workshop list this as a major contributor to anger and loss of control, which leads them to being rude and uncharacteristically uncivil. Many will note their inability to master even the phone system, not knowing how to transfer people without cutting them off—and then they have to learn yet another software program for their computer. It is a common complaint, but people are not fully aware of the depth of their reactions to technology until they discuss it.

Of course, technology was supposed to have solved all our problems and made our lives easier. In many cases, unfortunately, what machines did was to replace the people who used to assist us, putting "lean and mean" efficiencies in their places. Many administrative personnel were eliminated, and professionals found themselves wearing more hats—you not only had to research and produce reports, but you had to type them as well. This came at the time when it seemed that everything suddenly had to be ready yesterday. For older workers who had to give up their secretaries (and their yellow legal pads) almost overnight, the level of confusion and stress was staggering.

Doing more with less causes unchecked incivility. A common complaint in my workshops is that one has to wear ten hats and do ten jobs—and "Do it fast. Do it now." Planning and patience seem to be virtually unknown. This leads to stress, which produces the shoving, yelling, and phone slamming now so common in the workplace. When people feel disrespected, it becomes a very potent trigger for rage.

With technology, our increasingly global workplace has become more fragmented as well. Some workers are telecommuting, others teleconferencing, and most communicating by e-mail. A human element is missing in all this, which makes developing interpersonal relationships more difficult. Given the lack of tête-à-tête in today's business milieu, it is easier to "flame" someone via e-mail. When I have confronted people who have been rude to me over e-mail in subsequent telephone conversations, they do apologize, but say that I did not understand the tone of the e-mail. Because e-mail has no voice inflection (and, of course, no body language), people can use technology as a shield for rudeness. But even if rudeness is at arm's length, isn't it still rudeness?

In fact, technological advancement has facilitated the spread of incivility. Few people reflect on what they have written before sending an e-mail, as they would have before mailing letters, or give much thought to the content of a voice-mail message. Communication that used to be composed with deliberation and forethought is now produced instantly, without benefit of any second thoughts. Furthermore, the impact of rude missives is magnified greatly by new technologies. E-mails, for example, are usually copied to several people, and many innocent people might feel the sting of rudeness that was directed at the primary recipient.

Expectations about what machines will enable us to do are often unrealistic; for most machines to work, they need human contact. Overreliance on technology in an office produces a superficial, mechanical approach to work that encourages the subordination of human needs to information technology. The expression "24/7" has become all too common in corporate life. You are expected to remain plugged in at all times, even when you are sick or on vacation. It is not surprising that this frenetic pace quickly burns us out.

In Summary: We're Still Accountable

In attempting to explore and understand the evolution of incivility in our world and thus in the workplace, I am not implying that we should be exonerated for our rudeness. The ultimate responsibility rests on our individual shoulders to behave in a civil manner and promote that kind of behavior in others. We must look beyond the culture of blame ("It's not my fault!") and honestly appraise what we are really about and what type of individuals we want to be. Do we really have so many demands on our time in the 21st century that we have to give up accountability? Or is it that we are disorganized or just cannot be bothered? Or do we simply feel that no one cares, so why make the effort?

If we cultivate the necessary self-discipline, we do not have to blindly follow the dictates of the environment and the marketplace. We can achieve a measure of inner tranquility and impart it to others. If we know in our hearts that our strength comes from thinking, saying, and doing the right thing—not because it is dictated by the law, but simply because it is right—we will become personally responsible for civility in our lives. (Even remaining calm when someone cuts you off in traffic is a first step that can be replicated in the home, the community, and the workplace.)

Personally, the rewards are simple, yet gratifying—better sleep, wellness, a happier disposition, a better family life, lasting relationships with substantial friends, more productivity, and a healthier outlook toward life. All these assets contribute to a longer, happier life, a third of which we spend at work. We may as well make that component enjoyable because it impacts the other two-thirds so enormously!

For the business community, as we will explore in detail in the next chapter, there are considerable imperatives to overcome the civility crisis. Declining staff morale and productivity, costly employee turnover, ebbing customer acquisition and retention patterns, lawsuits, and negative publicity are some of the problems that can be avoided through an effective civility program.

One necessary step is to alter our tolerance threshold and let people know how we expect them to behave and what we will not tolerate. Ultimately, it is our choice. We can choose to behave in a civil manner because it brings inner peace and respect from others. When you treat people well, you likely will receive similar treatment. The reciprocal aspect of civility is a wonder!

CHAPTER 2

The Business Imperatives of Civility

"Today our talk is coarse and rude, our entertainment
is vulgar and violent, our music is hard and loud,
our institutions are weakened, our values are superficial,
egoism has replaced altruism and cynicism pervades."

—*A judge observing society in general in the Final Report of the*
Committee on Civility of the Seventh Federal Judicial Circuit, June 1992

In this climate, no one should be too surprised at the degree of uncivil behavior that has crept into our offices and organizations. Incivility in the workplace has grown to such crisis proportions that the business community can no longer ignore it. Individuals may choose how they want to behave outside the work world, but businesses cannot afford to allow them this same choice in the workplace. The risks of taking a passive stance toward bad behavior are too high. We need to learn how to create an open and effective work environment for a diverse workforce and to promote policies for treating everyone with respect.

A sense of quiet desperation exists among business leaders. As we will see in one benchmark study discussed in this chapter, nearly half of all employees have contemplated quitting because of experiencing uncivil behavior on the job—and fully 12 percent have, leaving businesses with an enormous bill for recruiting and training their replacements. The morale and productivity of many who stay decline, causing customer service problems that inevitably lead to a loss of clients. In our service-oriented economy, that is disastrous. Incivility-related lawsuits are a reality with which the business community must now deal, along with the bad publicity they can bring. And a demonstrated link exists between incivility and illness.

We will examine not only the problems pervading the workplace that argue persuasively for implementing corporate civility programs, but also some of the added benefits of doing so, such as reinforcing a value system, producing more competitive employees with better skills, and better preparing a staff to compete in a global marketplace.

Civil versus Uncivil:
Research Shows the Costs of Incivility

So just what is civility? Civility has less to do with the formal rules of etiquette than with an overall concern about treating others in a sensible, understanding manner. Workplace civility in particular is behavior that helps to set and preserve standards. It consists of workers positively relating to one another, cultivating reciprocal respect, building relationships, and learning to identify with their colleagues.

Sensitivity is a component of civility, as is the ability to make others comfortable. For me personally, civility is being mindful of the dignity of the human being in your sphere, taking care not to demean that individual in any way. If you are the type of person who affirms others and values their unique traits and talents, you are on the right track!

Incivility, on the other hand, is bad behavior characterized by a lack of consideration toward others. Workplace incivility can entail physical, verbal, and nonverbal behavioral patterns in interactions with coworkers, as well as violation of such norms as collaboration and good communication that lead to a safe, pleasant, and productive environment for all. Epidemic incivility runs beyond issues of political correctness.

!@!%#!@!%#!@!%#!@!%#!@!%#!@!%#!@!%#!@!%#!@!%#!@!%#!@!%#!@!

Examples of Workplace Incivility

- Not returning phone calls, voice mails, or e-mails
- Shouting at someone, regardless of status
- Berating underlings in public
- Removing someone's area of responsibility without consulting him or her
- Belittling people who are different or think differently from you
- Habitually interrupting others
- Acting as though only your opinions count
- Setting impossible deadlines for your subordinates to meet
- Not recognizing everyone's strength in a group project
- Failing to acknowledge colleagues in the hallway
- Not keeping appointments
- Permanently replacing a woman who is on maternity leave with another worker

Research shows that unbridled workplace incivility has calamitous effects on business. In their celebrated study "Assessing and Attacking Workplace Incivility" (*Organizational Dynamics* 29, no. 2, 2000), Lynne Andersson, Christine Pearson, and Christine Porath interviewed a cross section of workers, including administrative staff, midlevel managers, plant supervisors, professionals, physicians, security staff, senior executives, and technocrats. Those interviewed worked at a variety of profit, nonprofit, and government entities. A full range of hierarchical positions from every standard industrial classification was represented and the data reflect a balanced sample by gender.

The results are eye-opening! The researchers found that as a result of uncivil behavior at work:

- 22 percent of respondents intentionally decreased work efforts,

- 10 percent decreased the amount of time they spent at work (absenteeism),

- 28 percent lost time avoiding instigators,

- 53 percent lost work time worrying about the incident or future interactions,

- 37 percent reduced their commitment to the organization,

- 46 percent contemplated changing jobs to avoid the instigator, and

- 12 percent actually quit companies to avoid rude instigators.

These numbers are not only compelling, but tell this story: On-the-job incivility not only affects those who are involved directly, but also undermines an entire organization's effectiveness. I know that as soon as I make my first phone call to a company switchboard, I can tell if positive interpersonal relationships are valued there. As soon as I walk into an organization, I can tell what the civility quotient—or the measurable amount of civility that emanates from individuals—is!

The undesirable and often unrecognized consequences of incivility are many. Let's take a look at some of the more significant negative effects, starting with the findings of the Andersson, Pearson, and Porath research and my own practitioner observations.

Retention: Alienated Employees Are Expensive

Retention is the area most greatly impacted by unchecked incivility. Nearly 50 percent of respondents contemplated changing jobs and 12 percent actually quit. Employees may still cower when being yelled at by a superior in the workplace, but today they are educated about abuse and many may feel empowered to take action. They know that they can always go elsewhere if the going gets rough because of incivility in their present workplaces. The stigma of changing jobs often has disappeared—providing an escape to people in pain.

For the organization, however, alienated employees who jump ship are very expensive. Two independent consulting firms, Hewitt Associates and the Saratoga Institute, have estimated that the cost of replacing a worker runs between 1 and 2.5 times the annual salary of the job, and the more sophisticated the job, the higher the cost.

When an alienated employee quits, the organization faces a huge tab for recruiting a replacement candidate, flying him or her out for interviews, and paying for a move—perhaps across the country or halfway around the globe. And this situation doesn't include the work that doesn't get produced, customers who don't get serviced, and profit centers that stagnate while the position remains unfilled. Under these circumstances, it is difficult to build long-term, sustained success, whether in government, academia, private industry, or the not-for-profit sector.

To further muddy the organizational dynamic waters, the research indicated that in the case of incivility-induced departures, businesses may find it difficult to make the link between cause and effect. One reason is that some targets of uncivil behavior take their time when changing jobs, with significant time lapses between occurrences and departures. Others leave quietly, fearful of repercussions. In my own practice, I also find that employees may say nothing about incivility in exit interviews because they believe that their views would make no difference.

Sometimes management fails to identify the real reasons why people leave. The departure may be chalked up as typical of the industry or of a fast-moving market. And if behavioral harassment is covert, the Human Resources department is often totally in the dark. The only way to start building an awareness that harassment is taking place and work toward zero tolerance is to make civility an important criterion, ask direct questions in exit interviews, and follow through.

Previously, people who reported incidents of incivility were considered hypersensitive, although that response is slowly becoming less common. Awareness of incivility as a workplace dilemma that causes pain for everyone involved remains a vague perception. It is where child and spousal abuse and sexual harassment were 30 years ago—everyone knew they existed, but because these were not easily understood phenomena, they were ignored or denied.

According to Professor Andersson, who is now at the University of Western Ontario, and her fellow researchers, incivility can be ambiguous when intent to harm is taken into consideration. That is why it is more difficult to handle than acts of outright aggression.

While I agree with this assessment, I would add that from a legal point of view, an instigator's intent to harm is irrelevant. It just becomes a way for employers to excuse bad behavior. One cannot possibly enter into an instigator's mind and determine whether he or she intended to harm his or her target. We have to concentrate on the evidence—the instigator's words and deeds.

Some types of incivility are clearly more obvious, such as yelling and screaming, fist pounding, and spitting. Others are more subtle, such as undermining someone's work, being unreasonable in providing vacation days and bereavement leave, and constantly making minor but irritating putdowns.

Furthermore, people differ about their perception of acts of incivility directed against them. Diversity is not only about skin color, the shape of one's eyes, and gender. It is also about how we interpret feelings and react to situations. For many, it is humiliating and troubling to be on the receiving end of uncivil behavior; something as seemingly trivial as not having a phone call returned can be troubling. For others, who might have grown up in homes where such behavior was accepted, even being yelled at may not be so demeaning. But does this mean that we all have to develop thick skins and put up with incivility?

One important analytical tool is to look at retention by demographic group. If the turnover rate varies greatly among demographic groups (and the same measure applies to tenure rates and job offer refusals), this can indicate that the organization's criteria for respect are wanting. Women and minorities in general tend to place a greater emphasis on respect-oriented issues, and some subcultures hold civility in even higher esteem than others. Among white males, according to personal observation, those who possess more conservative values along with a sense of social justice are more likely to embrace and practice civility.

Diversity means you have to reach out! According to the U.S. Census 2000, by 2010, racial and ethnic minorities will make up 31 percent of the workforce and by 2005, fully half the workforce will be women. Clearly, businesses must make sure that civility is a part of their core values and practices before they alienate even greater numbers of employees.

Productivity and Morale: Why Bother?

Incivility creates an unpleasant work environment where people simply stop doing their best—and sometimes stop doing at all. When relationships among employees are unraveling and management ignores the problem, workers stay away more often. Absenteeism climbs and productivity plummets. Who wants to spend time in an unpleasant environment? Those who do show up work less effectively because they're fretting over uncivil encounters and worrying about the next interaction with the instigator.

I have been told by targets of uncivil behavior that once relations sour, targets will go to great lengths to avoid instigators, rerouting paths to avoid hallway encounters or withdrawing from task forces. This cannot help but generate a toxic atmosphere in which valuable on-the-job productivity diminishes rapidly. The targets experience numerous adverse effects; the job, job satisfaction, supervision, peer relations, and life in general all suffer. Life becomes a "drag." Professor Andersson says that at that point you start thinking only of whether you will "fight, flee, or take care of 'me'."

Some U.S. American corporate cultures tolerate incivility because they believe that it boosts production—this despite a body of research to the contrary. In fact, increased production demands come with heavier workloads, coupled with longer hours. All of which increases workplace incivility, which in turn diminishes output. Camaraderie and cooperation are the bases of productive work environments. Sure, healthy competition is beneficial, but the operative word is healthy. Being competitive and respectful are mutually inclusive concepts.

When incivility is ignored, not only morale but also mentoring deteriorates. Corporate culture needs mentoring to sustain long-term success; if it is not passed down from worker to worker, the culture declines and disappears. This is an especially adverse development for those workers already working at a disadvantage. Without mentoring, women and minorities will never make progress in a majority's terrain. In the United States, that is white male territory, but in other parts of the world it might be the turf of men from a dominant tribe, ethnic group, language cluster, or religious sect.

Customer Service: Spiraling Downward

Victims of incivility sometimes take out their frustrations on clients, creating a ripple effect. People do not perform to their full potential after being mistreated by a supervisor or coworker, and, many a time, customers bear the brunt of the ill will. How many times have you gone into a supermarket or drugstore chain and been "helped" in a surly and most unhelpful manner? How many times have you called a bank's or a post office's customer-service line only to be treated rudely? Or been snapped at in a hospital or hotel? Or had the doors closed on you in the public-transport system? Wonder why? It's quite possible you are experiencing the results of an uncivil work environment!

Sometimes an employee will actually vocalize discontent with a customer. I have had this happen on numerous occasions. These victims of uncivil behavior do not know who I am, but they need to talk to someone about the behavior of a mean-spirited leader or an incident of disparagement.

Customer Acquisition/Retention: Easy to Lose, Hard to Come By

Once the general public starts to hear tales about a company's inattention to civility in the form of workplace intimidation, harassment, and rudeness, it will desert in droves. No matter how rude we may be as a society, we won't tolerate rude service. When we pay for a service, we want it to be delivered graciously and civilly. But when the work environment is uncivil, the ripple effect invariably spills over onto the customer base. Once customer service erodes and your company gets a reputation for incivility, you lose market share. Study upon study demonstrate that from 58 percent to 62 percent of customers take their business elsewhere after encountering rude behavior.

Regaining consumer confidence after such a loss is not only excruciatingly difficult but extremely expensive as well. Acquiring new customers is a gigantic task even without having to overcome a negative image in the process.

Why do you think that a business such as Southwest Airlines, which has a superior reputation for customer service, is constantly conducting surveys about civility, which in their corporate culture is referred to as "kindness"? They use the results to incorporate new modules into training programs and make their environment and their service even better!

Lawsuits and Negative Publicity: Is Defending the Instigator Worth It?

Targets fight back against the company, not the tormentor. Remember that. If you ignore the problem, it could cost you plenty—more than just the money lost in a lawsuit. Is the negative publicity worth it? Is an employee babbling to a client worth it? Is jeopardizing a human being's health worth it? Is your troubled conscience worth it?

In another chapter I talk about conflict management and show how some organizations are providing alternatives to lawsuits and substituting goodwill for litigation. For now, let us look at one of the U.S. corporate community's darkest secrets— the thousands of lawsuits that are brought against businesses be ause of incivility. Some of the plaintiffs sue for "emotional distress," others for an organization's having created a "hostile environment."

One of the cases that is considered a landmark in incivility is *GTE Southwest, Inc. v. Bruce*, 998 SW 2d 605 (Tex 1999), in which three employees sued their employer for intentional infliction of severe emotional distress based on the workplace conduct of their supervisor. The court defined emotional distress as "all highly unpleasant mental reactions, such as embarrassment, fright, horror, grief, shame, humiliation, and worry." Severe emotional distress was defined as "distress that is so severe that no reasonable person could be expected to endure it."

Texas courts (this case took place in Texas) have held that a claim for intentional infliction of emotional distress "does not lie for ordinary disputes." The court said an employee "must prove the existence of some conduct that brings the dispute outside the scope of an ordinary employment dispute and into the realm of extreme and outrageous conduct."

The employees produced evidence that over a period of more than two years, the supervisor, Shields, engaged in a pattern of grossly abusive, threatening, and degrading conduct. These are some of the episodes, taken from the court testimony and corroborated by witnesses, that the employees suffered:

> Shields used vulgar language such as f--k and mother-f---r as part of his normal pattern of speech. When he was asked by employees to curb his language, he would position himself in front of their faces and scream, "I will do and say any damn thing I want and I do not give a s--t who likes it." On one occasion, when a plaintiff asked him to stop using expletives because the female employees did not like it, he said, "I'm tired of walking on f----g egg-shells, trying to make people happy around here."
>
> One employee testified that Shields would call her into his office every day and make her stand in front of him, sometimes for as long as 30 minutes, while he simply stared at her, talked on the phone, and read papers. She was not allowed to leave the office until dismissed.
>
> Once when Shields discovered a spot on the carpet, he had an employee get down on her hands and knees and clean the spot, while he stood over her screaming. The employees had to vacuum their offices daily, despite the fact that the company employed a cleaning service.
>
> On an occasion when one of the three employees forgot her paperwork, she was made to wear a Post-it note on her shirt that said, "Don't forget your paperwork."
>
> Evidence was presented that Shields would "lunge" at the employees, stopping uncomfortably close to their faces while screaming and yelling.

Shields's ongoing acts of harassment, intimidation, and humiliation and his daily obscene and vulgar behavior, which his employer defended as his "management style," went beyond the boundaries of what is considered tolerable workplace conduct. The employees complained that severe emotional distress manifested itself "in the form of tension, nervousness, anxiety, depression, loss of appetite, inability to sleep, crying spells, and uncontrollable emotional outbursts," and sought medical and psychological treatment for this suffering.

The jury considered the conduct as a whole and found for the employees. Later, the Supreme Court of Texas affirmed the decision after appeals saying:

> Occasional malice and abusive incidents should not be condoned, but must often be tolerated in our society. But once conduct such as that shown here becomes a regular pattern of behavior and continues despite the victim's objection and attempts to remedy the situation, it can no longer be tolerated. It is the severity and regularity of Shields's abusive and threatening conduct that brings his behavior into the realm of extreme and outrageous conduct. Conduct such as being regularly assaulted, intimidated, and threatened is not typically encountered nor expected in the course of one's employment, nor should it be accepted in a civilized society.

The judges said they had examined the "totality" of the case and affirmed the jury's award to the plaintiffs of $275,000 plus interest.

My research led me to countless lawsuits around the country regarding behaviors that shocked me, even though I thought I had heard all the horrific stories in my workshops! In one of the most appalling, *Qualicare, Inc. v. Runnels,* 863 SW 2d 220, 223 (Tex 1993), evidence was produced that a supervisor had made repeated threats and phone calls, placed the employees under surveillance, and sent a black floral arrangement as a death threat!

Thousands more cases of uncivil behavior exist that are less dramatic than the case involving the black floral arrangement, such as threatening job loss. They just don't receive much press in a society that does not value civility to begin with. I once worked for an insurance firm whose founder wrote books about thinking positively. The organization was one of the worst possible places to work. The founder's son regularly screamed and yelled at the men who sold insurance or managed the sales force, who would just cower in their seats; some would stutter after the experience. It was sad to witness the mouth-foaming tantrums, constant belittling, and fist pounding by this supposed leader. He died from a heart attack shortly thereafter, way ahead of his famous father. Even his own body could not handle his stress! I could not tolerate the toxic environment and left the organization after a short period.

Not surprisingly in light of this discussion, one of the hottest new forms of insurance is employment practices liability, which has seen incredible growth over the past ten years. Organizations now need this insurance, unheard of before the 1990s, because of the burgeoning laws protecting people against various types of harassment and growing employee awareness of their rights. The insurance would be unnecessary if organizations just spent some time and money to cultivate more civil environments with better working conditions in the first place. An ounce of prevention goes a long way.

Employment practices liability insurance covers a long list of workplace abuses, such as infliction of emotional distress or mental anguish, humiliation, breach of covenant of good faith/fair dealing, wrongful deprivation of career opportunity, and nonsexual harassment, that would be applicable to some of the cases and examples just cited. (For more information on this type of coverage, contact <www.gnwinsurance.com>.)

Workplace incivility, especially the persistent and emotionally distressing behavior known as bullying, is receiving far more attention outside the United States, particularly in Europe. In 1991, the European Union (EU) passed a recommendation regarding Dignity at Work that stressed the entitlement of individuals to being treated with dignity in the workplace, whether they are employers, employees, or customers. "According to one of the articles in the book *Building a Culture of Respect: Managing Bullying at Work* (Noreen Tehrani, ed., Taylor and Francis, 2001): "This shifted the focus from a defendant's alleged breach to a victim's rights."

A recommendation from the EU usually persuades private groups and national governments to initiate action. The Dignity at Work recommendation has sparked considerable research in several member countries, along with consideration by various national parliaments. Sweden took the lead by outlawing bullying in the workplace in 1993. Since then, other countries, including Ireland, have formed multidisciplinary task forces to study the phenomenon. France has labeled such behavior "psychological/moral harassment" [EIROline (European Industrial Relations Observatory) country: France], and in June 2001 the French parliament passed a bill making bullying in the workplace punishable by a prison sentence of up to one year and a fine of $13,000. Critics of this bill say that only "downward" bullying is included. (Downward bullying is when people in authority abuse their power and berate subordinates frequently.)

As of this writing, the Portuguese parliament is considering legislation against bullying, labeling it "psychological terrorism/moral harassment" (EIROline country: Portugal). Both the French and Portuguese parliaments have stressed the need to safeguard workers' psychological integrity. Some of the examples of "psychological terrorism" cited are allocating tasks for which an employer is overqualified, moving workers to different locations to damage their career advancement, and making threats or insinuating comments to the worker outside the workplace. The French even recognize resulting health disorders caused by incivility as industrial illnesses eligible for assistance under the health system.

Health Disorders: Incivility Takes Its Toll

Given the attention that the Europeans have devoted to many of the issues of incivility in the workplace, it is not surprising that they have conducted more research on workplace incivility and on the link between uncivil behavior in the office and dysfunctional health than we have in the United States.

Sadly for me, many of these studies were published in Scandinavian languages, with English translations hard to come by. In my research, I have had to rely on a friend's secondary account.

These Scandinavian studies are likely motivated by the emphasis cultures in that region place on pursuing the ideal in society, personal interactions, and working conditions.

In the United Kingdom, where more serious incivility is referred to as "bullying," quite a bit of research on the subject has been conducted and attention has been paid to addressing the problem in a comprehensive way. Correlations have been made between incivility in the workplace and increases in mistakes and accidents (Noreen Tehrani, ed., *Building a Culture of Respect*). Because the link between bullying and dysfunctional health has been established, General Practitioners (MDs) in that country have many established guidelines to help people impacted by incivility.

In the United States, Professor Lilia Cortina at the University of Michigan in Ann Arbor was the lead researcher in a recent pioneer U.S. study, "Incivility in the Workplace: Incidence and Impact," that found a correlation between incivility and poor health in the workplace (*Journal of Occupational Health Psychology* 6, no. 1, 2001). This well-publicized research demonstrated that performance and profits are profoundly affected by the adverse effects of incivility on employees health. Like the Andersson research mentioned earlier, this shows that workplace incivility is not just a personal problem, but one that diminishes the effectiveness of the entire organization.

In this study, rude or uncivil behavior included such occurrences as being addressed in an unprofessional manner ("Little Miss Lawyer Girl"), being ignored, receiving little interest in your statements or opinions, and having your judgment doubted. The researchers concluded that incivility results not just in hurt feelings, but also in anxiety, depression, nervousness, sadness, moodiness, excess worrying, and increases in such minor illnesses as colds and flu. The study also demonstrated that health disorders are heightened by employees experiencing incivility but choosing not to report it or not being able to do so. In a personal interview, Professor Cortina commented, "Although one instance of uncivil behavior might appear trivial, those slights and indignities add up. They create low-level chronic stressors. It wears people down."

Many Human Resources professionals think of the explosive outburst by a leader as the most disturbing type of behavior with the greatest impact. In actuality, it is the everyday unseen, unobserved slight, the constant barrage—no matter how petty or minor—and the social exclusions that most negatively affect one's health. I have learned in my consultations and workshops that repeated derogatory remarks, recurrent disrespect, and continued denigrations can take a larger toll on the target individuals than occasional screaming and fist pounding. (Not that I condone this type of outburst.)

Professor Cortina's team found that employees who experienced rudeness scored higher on a psychological distress scale and lower on eight measures of work satisfaction and commitment. Although women were more frequently targeted, both genders became more distressed, dissatisfied, and distant from their jobs as incivility became more frequent. Surprisingly, the study found the impact on psychological distress more pronounced in men!

When I asked Professor Cortina about this, she said, "One possible explanation has to do with the fact that men generally experience less day-to-day hostility/harassment/degradation than women. As a result, when men are hit with uncivil behavior, it may be more unexpected and surprising, and they may not have as much of a repertoire of skills developed to cope with it. This could lead men to find the behavior more distressing than women (who may, sadly, be more accustomed to and thus less fazed by incivility). However, this interpretation is entirely post hoc and speculative. Further study is needed before we can draw firm conclusions."

This is easy to accept as valid. In my own work, I am typically called on by male managers to intervene and to establish civility competencies not because of complaints in their divisions, but after they have experienced personal encounters with incivility. Last year, for example, I received a call from a male leader who was distraught because a subordinate had called him a mother-f---r to his face. He was so traumatized that he could not sleep for three days! A normal reaction, but would he have been sympathetic to someone else from his department reporting the same behavior to him before he experienced it himself? This was his rude awakening to a major problem.

I have long made the connection between wellness and civility. I stress it in my seminars and find that participants frequently talk about their health disorders associated with incivility. The most common ailments I hear about are headaches, stiff necks, intense back pain, "the shakes," loss of sleep, lack of ability to concentrate, and always being "under the weather." This is just common sense, but it took the research by Professor Cortina's team to give this premise the backbone it needed, to be taken seriously in the United States.

We have to create civil work environments where unreasonably stressful behaviors and demands are not heaped on employees who are already handling the invariable day-to-day job stresses, along with deadlines, an increasingly competitive and fast-paced business world, and the challenge of managing with less help.

In addition to avoiding critical problems with employees and customers, lawsuits, negative publicity, and bad health (as if those aren't sufficient incentives to institute a civility program in any organization), there are other distinct advantages.

On the Plus Side: Reinforcing Values and Training

When you introduce a broad-based civility program, which includes competencies based on civility, you strengthen core principles and demonstrate to stakeholders how serious you are. If your organization has "Respect for People" as a basic principle, you will find that steps to banish uncivil behavior serve to reinforce organizational values and clarify expected norms of behavior. The logistics of implementing a civility program and

FIGURE 2.1   Interconnections and Disconnections

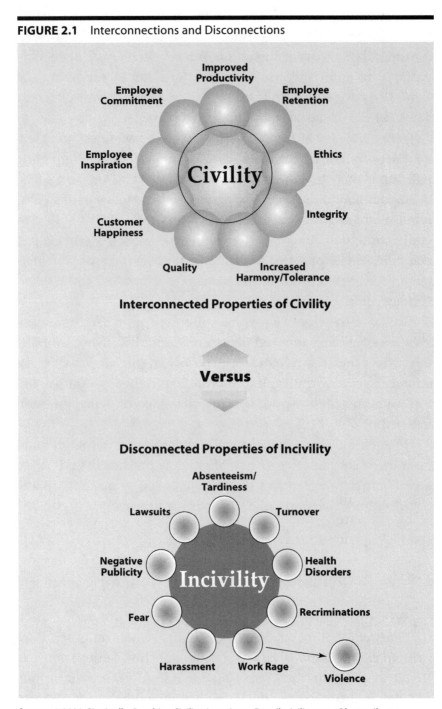

establishing civility practices as the norm will drive home your objectives and help a diverse group of employees find shared definitions and meaning to incorporate in their everyday interactions.

In the case of training and development, a civility program helps build and maintain a value system regarding such issues as diversity, ethics, and sexual harassment. It has always surprised me that facilitators addressing these topics use the basic premise of "respect" as a central theme of their training, simply assuming that participants know what respect means to begin with and disregarding the fact that it can mean different things to different people or nothing at all!

We compartmentalize our values and training so much that a holistic approach is seldom initiated. We do not even converse in terms of linkages. By learning respect, we learn how to treat one another with more consideration; the links are made. Figure 2.1 shows the interconnectedness of civility and the disconnectedness of incivility.

When an organization introduces civility training with comprehensive modules emphasizing respect, this helps clarify the meaning, shapes a shared understanding among a diverse workforce, and builds support for efforts to change the corporate culture into one that is more tolerant, fair, equal, and humane, and with significantly fewer instances of behavioral harassment. Civility training also helps handle difficult people. In fact, it helps cultivate all the other "soft," people-oriented skills that have been ignored by training departments for the past 15 years or so—redressing a vacuum that has, in part, caused the challenges of today. Furthermore, civility training provides individuals the opportunity for professional development in an emerging area and will enhance their résumés.

On the Plus Side:
Preparing for a Global Workforce

If your workforce understands the fundamentals of respect, you are better prepared and positioned to compete in the global marketplace. I recently discussed this issue with officials of Royal Dutch/Shell Group of Companies (hereafter referred to as Shell), the energy and petrochemical company with offices in 120 countries, and with Sprint, the global communications provider, which also commands a significant international presence.

Spokespersons for both corporations agreed that building and maintaining brand presence globally requires developing a standard of behavior that goes beyond complying with the local law. It involves obtaining a good understanding of the local culture and treating the diverse components of that culture seriously.

Furthermore, this process of familiarization should be directed from within, with the help of "local guides," and should be free of the perspective, policy, and prejudices of the individuals, corporation, or country of origin of those learning the culture. The goal should be development of policies that nurture sustainability and incorporate long-term vision. This vision requires cultivating patience and crafting communication skills that are devoid of parochial sports metaphors, idiomatic expressions, and patriotic braggadocio.

Multinational workforces, in offshore posts and at home in corporate headquarters, should know how to behave in all facets of international business—negotiations, relationship building, customer acquisition, and vendor relations. The world has indeed been "CNN-ized." If you do something wrong in one country, it will affect your business and standing in another.

Civility in all its incarnations broadens an organization's global marketplace, not only enabling the company to recruit and retain a superior international labor force, but ultimately to gain greater global market share as well—simply because they understand how to respect people and how to avoid offending them.

On the Plus Side:
Harnessing the Power of Civility

Again, let me emphasize that we spend a minimum of a third of our lives in the workplace. Clearly, this impacts the quality of the other two-thirds of our lives. How we perceive our time at work will influence the quality of our time off. If we are not content in our work, we cannot be happy and productive in the many other facets of our lives.

It is always cost-effective to be proactive and put a program in place before you really need it. A civil work environment allows you to recruit better employees and maximizes the fullest potential of all your human resources. Instead of constantly putting out fires and dealing with people's emotional problems and complaints, your civility program will allow for a more pleasant and safer workplace, which, in turn, will exert a lasting influence on the lives of those who work there. As Sprint says in their *Quality Handbook,* "People deserve respect and exhibit far higher performance when they receive it."

Employees will have greater self-esteem and more self-confidence in all areas of endeavor. Their interpersonal skills will improve, and with a more polished workforce, the organization's image will be greatly enhanced. Civility influences employees' success because it differentiates them in a competitive market by modifying negative behaviors that distract from their performance, while nurturing positive behaviors that will be noticed and admired. This is the basis of commitment to quality and excellence.

Corporations that are downsizing, restructuring, merging, and going through takeovers must be especially sensitive to any increase of incivility and diligent to nip it in the bud. Aggressiveness and bad behavior can be costly. It is better to be "positively" aggressive in creating a work environment characterized by civility and respect. Business must stop thinking of civility as decorative. Incivility diminishes productivity and morale and produces a very real negative affect on the bottom line. Promoting civility is good business—civility is both nice and necessary. It should be an integral part of any strategy to achieve corporate goals, compete successfully in a challenging environment, and increase profits—in a humane way.

C H A P T E R   3

How to Teach a Civility Course in the Workplace

*Y*ou decide *it would be too stressful to drive on the "parking lot" express-way to your workshop. So you take a taxi, thinking that the ride will give you time to relax and regroup. But the cab is filthy and smelly. The driver is filled with anxiety that he vents through vulgar hand gestures to other drivers and excessive horn blowing. Workplaces vary, as do how people handle stress. His workplace—which is also yours for the duration of the ride—is certainly not very comforting or conducive to getting anything accomplished. In fact, it gives you a headache!*

You exit the cab, breathe deeply, and proceed to your session. You have arrived early to check whether the client has followed your instructions about room setup and equipment requests—usually only about half of what you asked for is on hand and you have to start scrambling. Everything finally in place, you have the room's temperature adjusted for the comfort of the partic-ipants and organize your slides and other visuals. While distributing the work-books, you observe the participants as they file in, looking dejected and forlorn. You cheerfully greet the stragglers, for no one has initiated a "good morning." Your workshop seems to be viewed by many, who project an atti-tude that you're about to waste their time, as punishment! (Based on the author's frequent personal experience.)

Unfortunately, this is an attitude many reluctant participants bring to training sessions of any type. After booking a trainer and "drafting" participants, many organizations do little to explain the purposes, objectives, and relevance of the session to the staff. Civility workshops face especially tough resistance, because attendees come convinced that they know what the session will be about—and convinced that it is a subject matter in which they're not interested.

One of the greatest pleasures of my work is watching that resistance dissipate as participants in my workshops realize that their preconceptions were wrong, that civility is not about spot etiquette training or patterned niceness, that they are not here to learn which fork to use or how to curtsey. Slowly, they begin to realize that civility is much broader than manners—that it is about how we treat one another. They learn that civility is not about surface social niceties, but about something much more essential that comes from within. Together, we revisit an aspect of our lives that has all too often been put aside or forgotten in the whirlwind of today's pressured world.

By the time participants leave, they possess a different understanding of their behavior and the ways in which it affects their coworkers. They have learned to be mindful of the dignity of the human being in their spheres. They have mastered the lesson cited by Professor Stephen Carter in *Civility—Manners, Morals, and the Etiquette of Democracy* (Harper Perennial, 1998): "We need to learn anew a simple inequality: the question of how we should treat our fellow citizens is independent of the question of how we feel like treating them."

Watching the participants in one of my workshops reach this stage of self-awareness is a long process with many steps. The leadership of their organization first had to grasp the merits of a civility program and the role of civility training. A needs analysis had to be conducted to tailor the approach to best fit the organization. And, of course, the participants had to be guided through various workshop exercises!

This chapter will explain some of the steps of assembling a civility course model, examining in detail the process of making a needs analysis and then "sitting in" on a sampling of workshop exercises. It is important from the start to recognize that implementing a civility program is initiating broad and significant cultural change throughout every aspect of the organization and its operations.

We all have to unlearn old habits in order to adopt new ones! Figure 3.1 traces the progression from acquiring knowledge to effecting change. Within a business, this undertaking demands an organizational development approach that involves the whole staff, from senior management on down. If everyone is on the same page with the same expectations, the training will be effectively launched and the program will produce results beneficial to all.

Overcoming Organizational Resistance to Civility Training: We Need It Now!

The most important criterion for civility training to take place is to acknowledge that incivility is a valid problem that must be addressed. Sometimes a trainer, Human Resources director, or other decision maker within the organization must courageously decide to push for instituting this type of training—especially if senior management is disrespectful to begin with! These executives must be made to realize that the "tough" leader who behaves well only at shareholder meetings and at the country club is a dinosaur. Leaders who bark orders at underlings, place unrealistic demands on staff, and encourage incivility because they think it instills a winning spirit are fast becoming history.

The many imperatives for implementing workplace civility programs are detailed in Chapter 2. For now, suffice it to say that the effective leaders have learned that leadership has little to do with flaunting power and everything to do with demonstrating responsibility. They know that the synergy and energy that move

FIGURE 3.1   Civility Behavioral Model

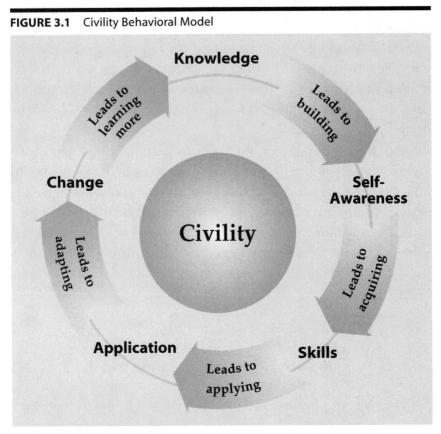

Source: © 2001 Giovinella Gonthier, Civility Associates. E-mail: civilityassoc@hotmail.com

an organization forward are determined by how well employees work together and by the very example that the leaders set. They know that workplace incivility can't be shrugged off because it affects the whole organization, not just the instigator and the target. And they know that civility training is not a "soft" skill to be dismissed, but one that will influence the bottom line in a very material way.

Other types of forces that need to be overcome in the organization are situational resistance because of habit and inertia ("Our present way of operating has always been good enough in the past."), opposition from those who think that they may lose power in any kind of shakeup, and plain old-fashioned cynicism from skeptics who mistrust human nature enough to doubt that training will produce improvement of any measurable sort. A strong case must be made that civility training presents a significant opportunity both for the business to grow and prosper and for the employees to be healthier and happier.

Some managers make the mistake of thinking that incivility only needs to be addressed in the lower echelons of the organization. Some executives try to exempt themselves from participating in training because they perceive their level of civility as commensurate with their status. The fact is that we all need to be conscious of raising our personal civility quotients. Even if we are not characteristically rude, we can all be inadvertently rude and need some skills to handle such occurrences. We can all fall victim to the spiraling societal forces and stressors that increasingly cause incivility and have led to well-publicized incidents of violence in recent years.

One of the most common problems that I encounter in my practice is the desire to train only one segment of an organization, such as line staff. What is the point of teaching an administrative assistant that a visitor with an appointment should not be kept waiting for more than ten minutes when his boss will subsequently keep the visitor waiting for an hour? When it comes to civility, there should be no obnoxious power inequalities. Morale is significantly higher and implementation more efficient if everyone in an organization, including senior officers, is required to take the training as a group. If senior officers are absolutely too busy, they should receive one-on-one coaching using the very same exercises that the rest of the employees have taken part in— but this can send the message that some folks are above the law and receive favored treatment.

Just as you must involve everyone within the organization in the process, you need a trainer from outside who is viewed as fair and impartial and who has not had disputes with other people internally. In-house trainers might have their own political issues with particular departments or employees and might not be the best people to do the training.

Step One: Do a Needs Analysis

The first step following the determination that an organization needs civility training is to conduct a needs analysis. You usually hear about such common manifestations of incivility as yelling, phone slamming, and profanity from the Human Resources staff and managers. But it is important to find out more about what the employees are experiencing in their daily work lives and also to determine their expectations.

Is there bullying taking place? Is a jerk protected and do his targets have to leave to get relief? Are there particular adverse circumstances that may be contributing to incivility in the organization, such as a staff shortage, or a space shortage that may have too many people crammed into cubicles with inadequate ventilation? Do workers have job security? Does the organization communicate important decisions to employees or keep them in the dark?

Needs Analysis Surveys: The Best Way to Tailor the Training

Because civility can be a touchy subject, I find that sending out surveys and then analyzing written responses is the best method for determining the depth of the problem at a particular site and developing a basis from which to design core modules. Established surveys designed to measure a broad range of issues, such as Employee Attitude Surveys, are more effective and reliable than an internally generated questionnaire on "civility." Those not aware of civility problems will treat too focused a questionnaire as a joke, and the targets of bullying may keep quiet because they fear being teased. A broader-based, independently administered survey will have greater credibility and will minimize the "social desirability response bias," which is the tendency to say what you perceive the organizational leadership wants to hear.

The best surveys I have seen are those designed by International Survey Research (ISR) (www.isrsurveys.com). (See Appendix B for a sample survey.) This group is expert in avoiding leading questions, designing easy-to-use questionnaires, imparting the importance of confidentiality, and monitoring changing attitudes and opinions over a period of time.

One useful case study is the analysis and monitoring by Shell, the European-based energy and petrochemical international business, in support of its "Respect for People" philosophy. (This is the same name that U.S.–based Sprint calls its civility program.) Shell, which has come a long way over the past several years in evolving its "Respect for People" approach, formed a "Respect" Project Team that reached these conclusions:

- "Individuals differ in what they understand about 'respect.' This is a consequence both of fundamental differences (culture, age, occupation, life experiences, etc.) and also different expectations."

- "Organizations are more than a collection of individuals. Organization values, rules, and processes impact leadership behaviors and the impact of 'respect.'"

- "Business and individual objectives are not always aligned. 'Procedural justice' and 'due process' are important factors in the perception of 'respect.'"

- "People are more than assets; [author's comment: Amen!] they are autonomous, and have personal accountability for their actions. The opportunity for dialogue, engagement, and involvement are all linked to respect."

The team also concluded that the best way to measure respect was by eliciting, in the overall attitude survey, a response to the statement: "Where I work, we are treated with respect." Using the word "we" was deliberate because "I" questions are disliked in some of the 120 countries in which Shell operates and also to give the opportunity to include situations in which a colleague was not treated well even if the respondent was.

Results of the civility section of an Employee Attitude Survey can be benchmarked against industry sector, national, and global high-performance norms with the available ISR database, demonstrating how well the organization is doing in relationship to competitors.

Verbal Interview Needs Analysis: Useful, but Time-Consuming

For smaller organizations on a tighter budget than Shell, who cannot afford to work with a survey firm, several other options are available. If the organization feels comfortable about providing the trainer an opportunity to conduct confidential one-on-one interviews with individual employees, the information obtained can be useful. Although holding interviews is cheaper than conducting surveys, this method is still somewhat expensive because it is so time-consuming. Unless the incivility problem is extreme, not many organizations opt for this approach.

Focus Group Needs Analysis: More Cost-Effective

Another possibility is to ask the Human Resources department to set up focus groups. Care must be taken to organize this appropriately, because power variable issues may be at work relating to civility. I usually suggest separating senior management and other managers and those they supervise into separate groups. Remember that management's interpretation of a problem is almost always different from that of line personnel, and you want participants to feel free to express themselves.

A good facilitator will be able to elicit information from the members of the focus groups that will be useful in gathering data for customizing training sessions. Assigning eight people to a focus group is ideal, which saves quite a bit of time over the individual interview method. This will give the trainer a good pulse on the issues and the group a sense of ownership in a course they helped to design.

One word of caution: You need to take your time and allow group participants to digest, think about, and respond to ideas. The group should not feel hurried, browbeaten, or controlled. Corporate training these days tends to be so rapid-fire it makes employees feel assaulted and actually contributes to incivility. Speed does not equate with quality!

"Parking Lot Boards" Needs Analysis: Ideal for the Smallest Organizations

Here's a method that may be effective for very small businesses. Every day a different question/statement is put up on a flip chart positioned outside the cafeteria, and workers are asked to submit anonymous answers on Post-it notes. The instructions on the flip chart state that the answers will be processed by an independent facilitator and the issues raised incorporated into the coursework for the training session.

Choose statements such as "We treat each other with respect here" or "People have left this company because of mistreatment." Once again, you are encouraging people to buy into the program through their input.

Observation Needs Analysis: It's Amazing What You'll See!

One of my favorite methodologies, which provides an excellent grasp of the civility environment, is to observe various areas in the organization incognito for three or four hours. I usually request a company pass that enables me to move about as an employee, not as a visitor, and always walk around on my own after obtaining directions to critical common areas. I try to break up my watch and vary the schedule—maybe putting in two hours one morning, an hour one afternoon the following week, and another hour two weeks later.

I make it a point to linger in the reception area, visit the bathroom (I have a male colleague visit the men's room), and hang around the break room or spend some time lingering in the cafeteria (good places to assess the level of respect for others). A definite must is to walk around hallways that pass by both private offices and cubicles. If people in the organization tend to shout expletives, slam down phones, or yell at customers or coworkers, I am able to scrutinize it and make mental notes. If rumors are a problem in the organization, I hear the rumors on the tour and find out how they are spread. (The bathroom is a major avenue for that!)

Usually, I can instantly tell whether employees are being productive or wasting time bickering over petty issues. And there is always a big difference between employee behavior on the job and in a training class on civility. I had previously heard one woman, who insisted during a training segment on profanity that she never used expletives, swear up a storm when I walked by her office. Observing how people interact in hallways is always helpful; I can gauge how friendly (or not) a place is by seeing if anyone ever asks me if I am lost or need assistance.

Making an observational analysis, you see things that supervisors and Human Resources personnel cannot see, because they are known and people behave differently in front of them! For example, this is how I witnessed a man brushing his teeth at the watercooler, as reported in Chapter 4. Most important, you can relate to issues participants raise in their classes because you have shared their daily experiences. When a trainer is able to resonate with trainees, you get a symbiotic relationship I term "fluidity," and nothing is more gratifying for everyone involved!

Step Two: Formulate Your Objectives

The next step is to formulate a set of learning objectives for the training session, based on the results of your needs analysis and consultations with key personnel. Be sure to include the objectives in the course workbook; participants like to know at the onset what knowledge they will be acquiring.

!@!%#!@!%#!@!%#!@!%#!@!%#!@!%#!@!%#!@!%#!@!%#!@!%#!@!%#!@!%#!@!%#!@!

Sample Objectives for a Civility Course

In our civility workshop, you and your teammates will:

- Discover the three Rs of civility (*personal, professional, and social responsibilities*).
- Define and identify incidents of incivility in the workplace.
- Analyze how you should treat people rather than how you feel like treating them.
- Examine "in-character" and "inadvertent" rudeness.
- Distinguish between "instigator" and "target" characteristics.
- Defuse anger/conflicts that destroy morale and productivity.
- Learn to normalize a relationship that has soured.
- Build listening skills.
- Develop ways to apply civility in the office immediately with more effective time-management/organizational skills, so phone calls and e-mails do not go unanswered and reports are handed in on time.
- Minimize profanity.
- Internalize the benefits of civility regarding wellness and quality of life in your daily situations.
- Build an atmosphere of mutual respect that helps with retention and productivity.

!@!%#!@!%#!@!%#!@!%#!@!%#!@!%#!@!%#!@!%#!@!%#!@!%#!@!%#!@!%#!@!

Continued

- Improve the balance of organizational conditions that facilitate or inhibit incivility.

- Facilitate the comfort and happiness of others—learn to be considerate and have a sense of duty. You will learn to handle people with diplomacy and tact!

And you will gain:

- A clear awareness of the impact of your appearance, attitude, and actions on your relationship

- A bright vision of your personal best

- Confidence

- The knowledge that ensures that you stand out as a top-quality person of distinction

- Behaviors that make you a world-class executive comfortable in any setting

Remember to tailor the objectives to meet the organization's unique needs. They should never be one-type-fits-all. The challenges differ within the same corporation from one site to another because of managerial differences and cultural variations. People in one regional office may well have a different understanding of and approach toward the concept of civility than those in another region, much less those in another nation.

When I was brought on board to put a program in place for one large multisite law firm, I found that their Washington, D.C., office did not need a grounding in civility as much as their Chicago and Denver locations did. The Washington firm routinely dealt with top foreign and domestic government officials and knew how to treat clients with dignity. Their hiring practices also were consciously geared toward employing people who valued civility. Prospective employees were actually asked during the interview process about their thoughts on civility and their experiences in dealing with people from different backgrounds and cultures. Senior management told me that one of the ways they judged candidates was whether interviewees addressed people they had just met by their first names before asking for permission to do so. It is a simple test, but sufficient. In that environment, a huge potential deal could be lost if a prospective client was disrespected in that manner from the start.

Step Three: Design Workshop Exercises

Now it is time to address the instructional exercises that will meet the training needs you have identified and the objectives you have set. Space will not allow me to share all the exercises that I have created for my own training workshops, but a few key examples follow. See the order form at the back of the book for information on how to order my workbooks, which contain numerous exercises that may be applied in a variety of situations, and the teaching manual to accompany them.

Before the class begins, I always review with participants the rules previously sent to them. It is critical that they turn off their phones, pagers, and palm pilots. Phone calls during a training class are disruptive! Tell participants that there will be breaks to check messages and that they are expected to return from breaks on time. Take attendance. Post a note on the outside of the classroom door asking anyone who arrives more than 15 minutes late to reschedule. Then close the door. (At one of my sessions, the CEO asked if he could personally read the rules to everyone. Hard to believe, but when an employee's cell phone rang about an hour later, the person left the room to take the call. The CEO promptly got up and locked the door so the offender could not re-enter. This CEO demonstrated that there are consequences to your actions!)

In my workshops, I use a minimum of technology, especially PowerPoint, because I want people to face each other and not a screen most of the time. I insist that participants sit in a u-shape configuration, not in rows classroom-style. This makes the subtle point that we need to learn anew how to respect people and not machines. As a facilitator, I encourage lots of interaction and urge participants to direct their comments to each other and not just to me!

Exercise One (Two Hours): Revisiting the Meaning of RESPECT

Based on the feedback I get through evaluations, this is the favorite exercise of many of my participants. It's my opening act and icebreaker. From the moment participants hear the musical tribute to respect playing in the background, they know this is not just a course about drinking tea with raised pinkies! It is also a valuable tool to facilitate people's ongoing awareness of their own behaviors long afterwards. This exercise fulfills many of the objectives mentioned in the sample objectives list on page 55.

Goal: To underscore behaviors that are causing pain in the workplace, but that are being overlooked, tolerated, or enabled.

Teaching Ideas: This exercise is interactive and experiential. Ask provocative, open-ended questions. Go all out and have fun with this one! People find it useful to associate acronyms with learning. Ask participants to name behavioral characteristics they associate with each letter of the word *respect*. You may want to use a flip chart and ask selected participants to write the answers on the chart while they are discussing respect; the rest can be writing in their workbooks (see Figure 3.2). Expound on each word that is volunteered. Follow up about why certain behaviors are issues (such as not returning phone calls). The answers will give you a chance to develop points related to areas identified through the needs analysis that require help.

The concept of "restraint" is important here—treating others how they should be treated and not how we feel like treating them! Introduce this notion if participants don't come up with it. "Ethics" is also a common characteristic mentioned. Ask participants what ethics means to them. You'll get both positive and negative answers that will enable you to probe further. "Colleague" is another popular response. What is a colleague? If people raise barriers or keep you from working effectively, are they colleagues? What are our obligations to a colleague?

Give participants free rein to talk. You'll be amazed what you hear! In one session when we got to "S," a woman proclaimed, "We have to slow down!" She went on to highlight most of the civility problems in the organization and to connect the dots between cause and effect! This was all the more powerful because it was heartfelt and volunteered spontaneously by one of the troops.

Another time, during a discussion of "Punctuality," mention was made of a chronically late receptionist who recently left the organization. One participant piped up, "Yeah, that really bothered me." I responded, "Why is that? How did his lateness impact on you?" The story unfolded that the individual, a supervisor, couldn't get her own work done because she always had to fill in for the tardy receptionist. The next step was to probe how this made her feel angry and how she sometimes took the anger out on a variety of coworkers. None of the parties involved are likely to forget these lessons quickly!

My classes may seem rigid because I set boundaries from the beginning. But once the classes get going, they are lively, interactive, and exciting. They really are! I tell participants funny stories about my time as a diplomat and all the faux pas that I saw—and include some of my own mistakes. We have some good laughs, but we are learning all the while. You should sprinkle your own anecdotes through your exercises. And remember that learners respond to trainers according to the way they are treated.

FIGURE 3.2   Sample Workbook Page—RESPECT

When we talk about RESPECT, what do we think of? What behavioral characteristics are associated with each letter? What behavioral traits do we exhibit? Some possible answers have been provided below.

R = RSVP to invitations, phone calls, and e-mails/Regard all people well/Reciprocate kindness/Restraint/Responsibility/ Recognition

E = Ethics/Expectations/Elegance in appearance

S = Stop, Slow down before we blow ourselves up/Serenity/ Standards/Security/Sarcasm avoidance

P = Patience/Punctuality/Performance/Procedural justice/ People are not assets

E = Excellence/Eye contact/Empathy/Equality/Ergonomics/ Empowerment

C = Consideration/Commitment/Clarification/Concern/ Cooperation/Colleague/Consultation/Conflict management/ Civility

T = Thank-you notes/Thoughtfulness/Teamwork/Timeliness/ Trustworthiness

Source: © 1998 Giovinella Gonthier, Civility Associates. E-mail: civilityassoc@hotmail.com

Exercise Two (One Hour): Ethics

Goal: To help participants understand ethics and give them the tools to work with if they are faced with a work-related dilemma.

Teaching Ideas: Many employees have no idea exactly what ethics means, so we start with defining ethics. To get the discussion going, I mention a few ethics policies from other organizations, as well as learning tools that some companies have put together, such as the Sprint ethics quiz on page 145. This often leads to a discussion about why some organizations do not have an ethics policy—and how the lack of a policy might impact an organization.

I provide newspaper articles about businesses and individuals who have gotten into trouble because of workplace ethics violations. These newspaper clips usually focus on:

- Expense reports and time reporting not filled out correctly/ honestly

- Organizations who defraud the government on their contracts

- Employees who maintain secret bank accounts for payoffs to keep the firm from being detected

- Trademark and logo violations

- Employees who steal inside information and pass it on, or who inadvertently pass on marketing and pricing schemes

- Nepotism issues

- Conflict-of-interest issues

- Drinking and driving while on company business

We discuss these items and then participants write about some possible scenarios in their own organizations in which an ethics dilemma could arise, such as someone stealing office supplies—or even a computer—for personal use. How would participants handle the situation? Volunteers read some of the scenarios to the class. Others relate what they would have done in the same situation. We talk about help lines and the benefits of having some mechanisms in the workplace to provide guidance.

Sometimes, I have the legal department give a brief talk about the costs to organizations and employees of possible violations. Frequently, I find that none of the organization's leaders has ever taken the time to discuss ethics with their own employees! It's quite a revelation. Organizations assume that workers know about this. Then we tie the ethics concepts we have discussed to respect and civility in general. People find it fascinating. They tell me that the "T" in RESPECT is for "Truth!"

Exercise Three (One Hour): Personal Stories

Goal: To minimize incivility in the workplace; define such pertinent terms as *instigator, target, bully, in-character incivility,* and *inadvertent incivility,* as well as inculcate listening skills.

Teaching Ideas: Too many workshops in the United States are tightly controlled. Incivility has caused a lot of pain in the workplace. And not giving people autonomy or variety in their jobs is a big reason for their rude behavior. So I try to vary methodology in my workshops and allow the participants some control through storytelling. I note that we live in a country with a rich storytelling tradition filled with contributions from Native Americans, Irish-Americans, African-Americans, and many others.

I encourage participants to share their personal stories about both acts of kindness and of incivility that they have experienced at their workplace. After each person has related his or her example, we examine a possible moral—appreciates others for kindness, has self-respect and will stand up for his or her rights, or values honesty or duty—or the negative side—someone bullies others or exhibits in-character incivility (intrinsically uncivil behavior).

Rich, personal traditions like storytelling are almost always ignored in corporate training in favor of fast-paced exercises with images flashed on a screen. Conversely, my approach reinforces how people should talk to one another, interact, listen, and empathize. Many communication and civility skills are being learned as the stories are told.

Once an Irish participant asked to get his guitar so he could play a tune while he recounted a bullying incident he once experienced in a ballad-style presentation. We then had an impromptu discussion about why bystanders (colleagues) can be apathetic and not assist a target. Why do we lack empathy? It was one of the best classes that I ever had because it generated so much passion!

This storytelling exercise has also fallen flat on its face a couple of times, I must admit—training is not about perfection. Too many dynamics are involved to constantly get it perfect. But you have to take the risk and persuade people to learn how to talk and listen to one another again! We are so accustomed to looking at a screen instead of each other in workshop settings and then going home only to flop on a couch and watch trash TV.

This is a good time for the facilitator to interject a minilecture, such as defining a bully, describing what a target is, or talking about attribution theory, which is all about the blame game—when you blame others for bad behavior but never consider yourself. Another minilecture topic is self-monitoring/impression management. The social scientist Mark Snyder, who is responsible for the self-monitoring theory, talks at great lengths about expressive control. People monitor their behavior for the sake of desired public appearances and are constantly concerned about situational appropriateness. If you are a social pragmatist, you learn to survive by utilizing patterns that impress in public situations.

Exercise Four (One Hour): Responsibility Awareness

One of the modules that I have found very effective in my civility courses and about which clients have raved is one I call the "three Rs." This exercise focuses on issues of responsibility and how to cultivate it.

Goal: To emphasize responsibility in all its phases.

Teaching Ideas: Start a discussion by asking the class to try and define what the three Rs of civility are. You are looking for answers in the areas of responsibility for oneself and one's actions (personal responsibility), responsibility for work (professional responsibility), and responsibility for others (social responsibility). You want the participants to feel responsible for more than just "me, me, me!"

Talk about what these concepts mean to them. How can they take responsibility for others in the workplace? Have them cite specific examples (supervising, mentoring, teaching, caring, cleaning up, etc.). Ask the participants whether there are times when all three types of responsibility apply concurrently. Ask open-ended questions such as, "How many of us take our professional responsibilities seriously?" or "What does it mean to be professionally responsible?"

Sometimes people go right to social relationships and never cover all three areas of responsibility. That's OK. Effective teaching is about capturing the interest of participants where it lies and not trying to force it on an arbitrary path. Adults are competency-based learners; they want to acquire knowledge that they can apply. So feel free to deviate from this module and take into consideration their rich experiences! If participants go on the relationship path, talk about the meaning of interpersonal relationships at work (approachability, warmth) and the opposite (arrogance, sarcasm, inflexibility). Ask how this fits into the three Rs of civility.

Be flexible. Remember that from your needs analysis you have an idea where pain is being felt in certain units of the organization. Without singling out anyone personally or naming any names, you can lead the discussion into these areas. You may want to add the following exercise from my workbook (see Figure 3.3), asking participants to fill in the blanks.

Another exercise that you may consider involves time management and organization abilities. This might be a no-brainer for older people who have been out in the workforce for a while or for those who have been in a particular job long enough to have developed a routine. For a younger person or someone who is not in a seasoned position, however, this can be very complicated. In my practice, I find that associates and entry-level managers have incredible issues with time management and organization abilities.

In the United States, we hire people based on how articulate they are and on their academic credentials, neither of which tell

FIGURE 3.3   Sample Workbook Page—Define the Three Types of
Responsibility

The world is a better place if we concentrate on teaching ourselves to be responsible. We feel more in control of our lives. Blaming others for our mistakes or actions drains a lot of energy and
creates rancor. Remember that when you point the finger at someone else, three fingers are pointing back at you!

Compassion, _____ , and _____ are defined as social
responsibility. How can we apply these in our workplace? _____
_____ .

(The answers for the above blanks can be "respect" and "empathy."
Doing our best at work is defined as _____
responsibility. Enumerate some of these responsibilities and how
you can do your best. What else would you consider as doing your
best? Look at the ways in which professionalism is interpreted in
your workplace. *Ask why we have trouble with this. (If people are
showing up late to work or are not being punctual to meetings, facilitate discussion in that area.) The answer to the above blank can be
"professional."*

To do the _____ thing even when no one else is watching is termed personal responsibility. Give a few examples of this
type of responsibility in general and as they apply to the workplace. *(If your company is experiencing common area problems such
as the copy room's fax machine never being refilled, lead the discussion in that direction.) The answer to the above blank can be "right."*

Source: © 1998 Giovinella Gonthier, Civility Associates. E-mail: civilityassoc@hotmail.com

us about how well prospective employees manage time and organization. These issues cramp their minds and crimp their production. When they cannot cope at work, the door slamming and
profanities escalate; this is their coping mechanism for lack of
certain skills. If that is the reason for incivility in the company,
incorporate a module on time-management and organization
skills such as filing systems and decluttering desks in the training; I usually hire an expert to come in for an hour during my session to work on time-management and organization skills.

I have provided a few modules and suggestions about how to teach a civility course. The exercises are just ideas for implementing the fundamentals of civility. Tailor a program based on your company's needs. There are countless more modules in my workbook (see the order form at the back of the book).

After instilling the core principles of civility, one can move on to such "spot etiquette" training aspects as phone manners, introductions and greetings, team interactions and dining etiquette. But remember, as I have said many times, spot etiquette alone is superficial and fails to instill the essence of civility.

C H A P T E R   4

Uncivil Behaviors
and Solutions

*Y*our commute by car the other day was nerve-racking, so you decide to try the train this morning. It is crowded, and at the third stop three young men in crumpled khaki pants board. As they adjust the shoulder straps of their laptop computer cases with hands sporting expensive wristwatches, they banter about how "the weather s--ks because it's too f-----g hot and who needs this s--t anyway." Meanwhile, the woman sitting next to you talks loudly on her cellular phone, mostly leaving messages informing the world that she is on the 8:05. When finished, she turns her attention on you and proceeds to relate a weird sexual dream from the night before. Now that reading your newspaper in peace is impossible, you put on a glazed smile, grit your teeth, and stare into space hoping to arrive at your destination soon. Why, you wonder, are no rules posted or separate cars set aside for cell phone users?

As soon as you enter your office, you witness another employee brushing his teeth at the watercooler in the hallway. Instead of screaming, you proceed to your office, feeling relieved that you have an office and not just a cubicle— at least you can close the door. You listen to your voice mail. A colleague wants you to call the consultant who the two of you talked about yesterday and leaves a rapid, garbled phone number. Deciding not to replay the message repeatedly in a vain attempt to catch the number, you call the colleague, who

of course is not in. A phone-tag scenario results. Another simple task has
turned complicated because of yet another person's inconsiderate behavior.
And the day was not going well to begin with. You boot up the computer and
start to scan your e-mail, finding none of the replies you were expecting and a
couple of snippy ones that you weren't! Welcome to the workday reality.

From intrusive cell phone conversations to rude e-mails, we're all experiencing a burgeoning range of incivilities during the typical workday. This chapter focuses on specific types of bad behavior that are causing the most ill will in the modern workplace, including those that can escalate into "rage." Many of these incivilities have been facilitated by the emerging new technologies that demand new rules just at a time when we seem to be losing our will to promulgate, enforce, or pass along any rules at all.

This is not a compendium of every bad behavior in the workplace, but an overview of issues and strategies basic enough to enable employees to take responsibility for solving problems themselves if supervisors do not address the issues. No two interpersonal situations are identical, and relationships are dynamic and ever-changing by nature. These scenarios may not apply exactly to the problems you are experiencing, but the concepts they embody are universal and should be adaptable to any workplace.

My examination is organized around negative behavior clusters that commonly cause workplace civility infractions, each with a suggested solution. You will likely recognize some behavior as exactly what goes on in your organization. Or you may be fortunate enough that after reading about these problems, you will exclaim about the place where you work, "Wow, it's not so bad here after all!"

TECHNOCOMMUNICATIONS
It's a New World Out There

The technogeeks and entrepreneurs of the high-tech market-place have sold us many nifty new gadgets that allow us to communicate in ways never before possible. Unfortunately, none of these "must-have" gizmos came packaged with directions on how to use them in a civil manner without infringing on the privacy and rights of others. They were unleashed into a marketplace already fraught with bad behavior without any caution about what might constitute inconsiderate usage.

Technogadgets are coming onto the market so fast that we need to reinvent manners for their use at a clipped pace. Far from being simply a boon to business, the new technology can, in fact, be the source of considerable frustration and a hindrance to office goodwill. But until someone in authority lays down the law, little is usually done to curb technoabuse.

Any good manager should realize that setting expectations elicits respect. Employees prefer to be told how they should behave at the outset rather than be constantly corrected as they blunder along. If you're a manager frustrated by technoabuse, start now with a new set of rules. If you're an employee, pass these suggestions along to the group leader for consideration.

Basic Telephones
Still Misused and Abused

Problem: Failure to listen and respond effectively

Solution: Telephone protocol is so simple, yet never taught and often bungled. We've been around telephones all our lives and just assume that everyone knows rudimentary telephone manners.

Most important, remember that the phone call is a two-way conversation. There is always a speaker and a listener, and these roles alternate. Once you have picked up the phone, devote your time to the other party for the duration of the call. Acknowledge this human being with respect and act in a manner that shows you care. In other words, pay attention and listen. Do not cut off people before they have finished their sentences. Bear in mind that few of us can listen effectively while multitasking; if you're typing, eating, surfing on the computer, or sending a fax on the other line during a conversation, you're probably not paying close enough attention.

When it is your turn to speak, be concise and always polite. Please do not whisper, shout as if the other party can't hear you, or try to talk with food or gum in your mouth. If you were listening to music when the phone rang, turn it off so that the listener can hear you without distraction. Measure your breathing so that the listener doesn't hear your every breath throughout the conversation. Pronounce words carefully so that the listener doesn't hear you "hissing." And do not grunt and say "Uh-huh" in response to every phrase.

And please remember that the office is a place where business is transacted; personal phone calls should be kept to a minimum.

Problem: People trying to show how important they are by holding multiple phone conversations at once, while you are on the phone with them—meaning they are answering second lines or holding another conversation on a cellular phone

Solution: Tell the self-important person who wants to treat your call like an airplane waiting for clearance to land that he appears to be occupied, and suggest that you continue the conversation when there is more time to talk!

Being put on hold is infuriating, especially when the holding periods are long. This demonstrates a pronounced lack of respect for your time. Sometimes the offender even makes you listen to the second conversation while you are on hold. This sort of behavior is like a virus; it spreads around to other people. Beware. Do you want to sound as frazzled as the perpetrator? Or as arrogant?

In some circles, it is in vogue to sound terribly busy, but, nonetheless, it is inconsiderate to treat other people on the phone this way. It is much better to devote a few minutes to the individual with whom you are talking and let voice mail pick up other calls. Polite professionals also do not juggle clients and colleagues with call waiting.

Problem: Answering the phone and saying you cannot talk

Solution: One current convention I do not subscribe to is opening telephone conversations by asking people you have called if they have time to talk. Once someone answers the phone, she should take the time to talk, period. (If you anticipate that it is going to be an unusually lengthy conversation, then it is correct to ask at the onset if the listener has a few minutes.)

If you can't take a routine call when your phone rings, don't answer it. That's what voice mail is for! Never put a caller in an embarrassing position by saying, "I cannot talk, I have someone in my office." If you have someone in your office, you shouldn't have answered the phone. Similarly, let voice mail take the call if you are on a deadline or busy with the budget; don't answer the phone and take your annoyance with the interruption out on hapless callers. How could they possibly have known? This is rude and unacceptable behavior.

Speakerphones
Little Redeeming Merit

Problem: Excessive use and concealing other people's presence in the room

Solution: Speakerphones make you sound distant and distracted, and are irritating to the caller. A courteous executive will use the speakerphone sparingly and always announce when one is in use; it is customary to apologize if you absolutely must use one of these gadgets.

If two professionals who have to review documents and take notes while negotiating a contract agree to use a speakerphone, that's a special circumstance and a mutual convenience. It is, however, advisable and courteous to intermittently pick up the receiver when you're not writing so you can converse more naturally.

If there are other individuals in your office when you use the speakerphone, always inform the party on the other end of the line and introduce all those who are in on the conversation. It's only ethical and polite to do so. According to protocol, if at least five or six people are participating, each should identify himself or herself whenever speaking.

The mute button is a two-edged sword. It is useful, for example, if you would like to filter out heavy construction noise outside your office but irritating if used so that someone can work on e-mail instead of paying attention to the discussion at hand. The delay infuriates everyone when the distracted participant suddenly chimes in and says, "I'm sorry. Can you repeat the question?"

Voice Mail
Would You Mind Repeating That?

Problem: Outgoing messages that are difficult to understand, incomplete, or inappropriate for the office

Solution: Always record a polite, professional, and understandable (in other words, speak slowly and clearly) greeting in your own voice (canned greetings are impersonal and may be confusing to the caller) for your voice-mail system. Omit cutesy greetings at work. Include your name, phone number, and necessary business particulars in a standard greeting. For special daily greetings, provide such details as the hotel name and a phone number where you can be reached that day, taking care to repeat the number during the message. If you cannot be reached, identify a backup contact if possible and indicate whether messages will be checked that day and when calls are expected to be returned—then return the calls as promised. When you are going to be away for an extended period because of travel or illness, provide particulars regarding when phone calls will be returned and when you expect to be back in the office.

Recording a message from a cell phone to your business phone has its pitfalls. Your voice can be cut off or the volume can be intermittent and then the message may sound odd.

If you cannot understand a garbled greeting, leave a message saying that the greeting was incomprehensible and ask the individual to please call back. Hopefully, these folks will take more care when next recording a greeting.

Problem: Incoming messages that are rapid-fire and incomprehensible

Solution: This is a frequent and extremely frustrating problem that wastes a lot of valuable corporate time. Employees should be trained to speak slowly and distinctly and to always leave a phone number twice to ensure that it will be understood.

If the call is internal, include your name, department affiliation, and extension in the message, stating the extension twice. If it is an external call, leave your name, company affiliation, phone and extension number, and a brief message. Repeat your phone number and extension. Never assume that someone has the number or should know it. The recipient might be out of the office or even out of town, without an address book available. Always leave your full name and not just "This is Susan"; the recipient might know five Susans.

If you receive a staccato message with an incomprehensible phone number and can at least identify the caller, e-mail or call back (if you manage to track down the phone number by another means), relating the problem and politely suggesting that the number be given twice in future messages. If you can't identify the caller, there's little you can do but hope the person calls back, in which case you can relate the difficulty the original message caused you.

Problem: Long, convoluted voice mails

Solution: Voice mail is designed for brief messages—generally, this means about 30 seconds or less. Just tell the recipient what you need and when you need it and sign off (remembering, of course, to slowly and distinctly leave your name and phone number, repeating the number). Longer and more involved messages should be sent by e-mail, unless the sender has a disability that prevents typing. (In that case, the disability should be mentioned at the start of the voice-mail message.)

Problem: Not returning voice mail

Solution: Voice mail should be returned within 48 hours. Not returning someone's call is tantamount to standing up that person. It is unbecoming and inexcusable and marks you as uncaring, disorganized, and rude.

If you are going to be out of your office for a while, leave a recorded message to that effect. If you find yourself perpetually falling behind in returning calls because of time management issues, seek help. If you do not want to talk to the caller at the moment, then ask someone else to return the call for you.

Voice-mail messages sometimes do get lost, so give the person you called the benefit of the doubt and feel free to repeat a call that has not been returned after three days. You will learn who is responsible about returning calls and who is not. My advice is never go into business with someone who does not return calls on a timely basis—it's too risky! And try not to choose such a person for your team at the office or for your volunteer committee.

Problem: Hiding behind voice mail

Solution: Calling after hours, during lunch, or at some other time when you know the person you are telephoning will be out of the office is all too commonly practiced by those late with a report, embarrassed over an unpleasant exchange earlier in the day, or leery of talking directly to a superior (it's an approach associates in law firms are notorious for employing to dodge partners).

In fact, all of us are tempted on occasion to hide behind voice mail—while we finish a project on deadline or cool off after a misunderstanding. But if this becomes a habit, you should be concerned.

The bottom line is that hiding behind voice mail is cowardly and will only make a bad situation worse. If you have a problem with someone, go to the individual's office and try to sort it out in person. If you are being bullied, abused, or harassed, go to the Human Resources department. If you are late with a report or a brief, call during normal business hours and explain the circumstances.

It is just as cowardly for large organizations to hide behind voice mail as it is for individuals to do so. Some companies make it especially difficult and irritating for customers to resolve problems and confound access to human customer-service representatives. You keep having to "press 2" for a solution and then are asked to "press 5" for other options that go on ad infinitum. You never get to a human being, and your problem remains unsolved. Many large phone companies, Internet service providers, and banks are notorious for using this poor customer-relations tactic.

Cell Phones
The Whole World Is Listening

Problem: Unnecessary, inappropriate, and disruptive use in public

Solution: Please turn off your cell phone while in such common areas as lobbies, corridors, rest rooms, or the office cafeteria, and while visiting someone else's office or at a lecture, luncheon, meeting, or training session. Extend your considerate behavior beyond the office to such places as the movie house, theater, restaurant, house of worship, classroom, or hotel public space, as well as on the sidewalk or on a bus, train, or plane.

Use a cell phone in public only for an emergency. If you expect a critical call, turn your phone to the vibrate mode, then leave the public space to take the call, if at all possible, or speak in a soft voice to avoid disturbing anyone else. Respect others' rights not to hear your conversation. Negotiating a business deal in public is strategically inadvisable anyway. Shouting out instructions to your broker while on a train draws unwanted attention to your portfolio and sets you up for potential fraud. Planning tonight's menu or rehashing last night's date in public is simply boorish.

The most egregious violation of cell phone usage in public that I have heard of in my practice was someone receiving a call on his cell during the funeral service of a colleague. And he took the call!

Problem: Forgetting to turn off your phone during an event

Solution: If you are reminded by the ringing of your cell phone that you have inadvertently forgotten to turn it off while in a meeting or at an event or a performance, quickly turn off the phone without answering it and apologize discreetly. (A savvy speaker will always remind the audience to turn off their cell phones at the beginning of the talk.) Even a mouthed or whispered apology demonstrates remorse.

Problem: A woman fumbling to find a cell phone in her purse while it rings and rings during a public event

Solution: Women often have a more difficult time with cell-phone etiquette because it takes them longer to get into their purses and find the phones before being able to turn them off.

Once you do get to the phone, turn it off without taking the call. Quickly and quietly apologize to the speaker and those around you. And next time, remember to turn off the phone before you go into a conference, a lecture, or someone else's office. If you are expecting an urgent call, turn on the phone to vibrate, put it on your lap, and sit at the back of the room near a door in order to make a quick, gracious exit. Refuse to look like a schoolgirl!

Problem: Conducting business on a cell phone while at a luncheon or dinner with clients or friends

Solution: This is ungracious and makes your clients or friends feel unworthy. A person who sacrifices his time to meet with you deserves the utmost attention without such distractions and time-wasting behavior on your part. Turn off your phone when dining and take a call only if you have to deal with an emergency—limit your definition of what constitutes an emergency. Cancel plans in a true emergency—the client or friend is going out to chat with you and not to listen to your conversation with someone else or sit staring into space while you are outside gabbing on the phone with someone else. Adhere to all club and restaurant rules banning the use of cell phones and stay with your guest the whole time you are dining. From a wellness point of view, a team in a crisis situation should take a break and eat in peace for at least 30 minutes without phones ringing. Conversations are more meaningful in calm situations.

Problem: Conducting business on a cell phone while driving

Solution: Wait until you get back to the office or at least have access to a regular phone. Talking on a cell phone while driving is distracting and can be dangerous to you and to other drivers. In the United States, several states now restrict cell phone use while driving. Even if you use a hands-free apparatus, the conversation can fade in and out, vary greatly in tone, and sometimes disappear altogether. This wastes time for everyone concerned.

Beepers
And the Beep Goes On . . . And On . . . And On

Problem: Once again—unnecessary, inappropriate, and disruptive use in public

Solution: People usually go out with these little devices prominently attached to their persons to draw attention to themselves.

They think it gives them an air of importance. In fact, it makes them look silly. Beepers are acceptable in some contexts, such as when worn by medical personnel in a hospital, emergency repair personnel, or managers who have widely dispersed teams they need to reach in a timely manner. In most other settings, beepers are annoying and their use should be tempered.

In public, turn the beeper to the vibrate mode and prepare to leave such settings as a theater or restaurant quietly and without disruption if the beeper goes off. Leaving beepers on at a play demonstrates an extreme lack of consideration for the actors. And when people dine out, they want to relax and not be disturbed by the sound of your beeper at the next table. Even in an office setting, emergency repair staff making service calls should set their beepers on vibrate so they don't distract nearby employees.

It also helps to inform folks that you are wearing a beeper and may need to leave. People are more tolerant if they know what to expect and that the disruption represents a genuinely urgent situation. At a dinner party, for example, a medical person should explain the circumstances to the hosts and the other guests.

Needless to say, the same protocol applies to watch and Palm Pilot beepers as well.

Problem: A man fumbling to find a beeper misplaced in a briefcase, a pocket, under a pile of documents—or heaven knows where—while the gizmo beeps away in the middle of a presentation

Solution: Just as women tend to bury their cell phones in the depths of their purses, men (who seem particularly fond of this form of technoumbilical chord) frequently misplace beeper apparatuses. Beepers are small and easily swallowed up unless uncomfortably affixed to your belt. If the "beep-beeps" start to emanate from a place of undetermined origin during a public presentation, quickly gather your belongings and look for the beeper outside the meeting room. Next time, turn on the beeper to vibrate, put it on your lap or a belt, and organize yourself more professionally. Show respect for the person speaking and for those assembled to listen. Refuse to look like a schoolboy!

Fax Machines
For Business Only

Problem: Indiscriminate or inappropriate use

Solution: Fax (facsimile) machines are useful for quickly sending some types of letters and documents. They generate hard copy that can be read and easily referenced; like e-mail, they're preferable to voice mail as a way to send any detailed information.

Faxes are very public, however, so be cautious. If you are sending something confidential, state this on the cover sheet. Don't send rejections, termination recommendations, congratulatory letters, love notes, thank-you notes, dirty jokes, an outline of your raised middle finger, or anything else personal or inappropriate for public consumption via fax. Always include a cover sheet to ensure that the fax is routed to the correct person and that any special needs such as confidentiality or urgency are noted.

Sensitive matter about a behavioral problem, someone's review, or confidential material such as that sent by a law firm to a client is better hand-delivered. If it is absolutely necessary to send material by fax to other than a dedicated line in someone's private office, ask the intended recipient to wait for it at the other end.

And never send advertisements over the fax—even as a marketing tool for your next seminar. (Sending mass distribution of unsolicited fax advertisements, sometimes called "fax blasts," is not only inappropriate, but may also be illegal.)

Fax machines, especially older models, can be temperamental. If you have any doubt that your fax was sent successfully, call and make sure.

Problem: Dialing the wrong number and sending sensitive documents to the wrong fax machine

Solution: Pay attention to the number that you are dialing; check it twice before pressing the send button. I have personally received detailed financial documents intended for someone else but sent to me mistakenly by a careless clerk or broker. If I were a thief, I would have had a field day with this material.

Problem: Dialing a regular phone number by mistake instead of a fax number

Solution: Pay attention to what you are doing. It is extremely annoying to pick up the phone and be greeted by a high-pitched fax squeal. To exacerbate the annoyance, the call is typically repeated three or four times before the caller figures out that he is dialing the wrong number.

E-mail
Easily Misconstrued and Often Ill-Conceived

Problem: E-mailing trivial information or brief messages to someone whose office is close by

Solution: Stop flooding the server needlessly. Face-to-face communication is still the best way to find out what's going on, solve any problem, create camaraderie, and spread goodwill. Hiding behind e-mail is antisocial!

Problem: Sending combative, complex, emotional, or ambiguous messages

Solution: E-mail does not have the verbal clues and nuances of telephone communication, much less the body language of a meeting in person. The medium is best used to convey fairly straightforward types of information rather than messages that could be misconstrued.

As noted earlier while discussing the evolution of incivility, e-mail tends to facilitate incivility because people hit the Send key with much less reflection than they would bring to writing and mailing a letter. Think about it and do not send an e-mail that you yourself would not like to receive. Many people send curt e-mails that could easily be construed as snippy (" . . . your reply by 5 PM is necessary. . . . ") and then hide behind the fact that their tone is difficult to pin down. Blaming the recipient for mis-interpreting a curt e-mail is unfairly turning things around. If someone takes offense at an e-mail of yours, simply say you are sorry and move on.

Problem: Sending sensitive information by e-mail

Solution: If you do not want it printed in the town newspa-per, do not send it via e-mail! Types of subject matter that should not be e-mailed include performance appraisals, sensitive strat-egy decisions, and your wish to terminate someone. Always deliver bad news face-to-face. And remember that it is easy to send e-mail by mistake with the click of a button. I have actually heard of memos recommending that someone be terminated being inadvertently dispatched to the person about to be fired.

Other types of e-mail that should not be sent from the work-place (or from your home to work colleagues for that matter) include those expressing religious or political issues and events.

Problem: Sending inappropriate or insufficient material by e-mail

Solution: Keep the office e-mail business-oriented and simple. Many people have neither the time nor the inclination to read your e-mail jokes at home—they really don't want to receive them at work, nor the details about Aunt Gertrude's surprise birthday party, nor a link to some Web site you found really interesting, connecting to which will sign them up for a year's membership. Nor is it appropriate to ask for pledges to your favorite marathon or other charities with which you are involved—unless your work-place is a charity and you are raising money to support your orga-nization's activities.

Remember that the more bells and whistles you load onto an e-mail, the longer and more laborious opening it will be. One colleague of mine wasted hours trying to clear his mailbox of photo scans someone sent him from a cosponsored event, which were too much for his system to open. If you want to attach bells and whistles, post the larger document on a Web site, providing a hotlink if readily possible.

Don't earn the justifiable ire of your correspondents by sending sloppy e-mails that leave out crucial details or forget to follow your "signature" with all the pertinent particulars, including your company's street address, phone, fax, and e-mail address (correspondents should be able to e-mail you without having to use the Reply key).

Of course, obscene or harassing use of e-mail and other communications technologies in the workplace and everywhere else is prohibited by law.

Problem: E-mails that go on and on and on

Solution: Be brief and get to the point. E-mails should generally not run beyond half the length of your computer screen. People want to determine the gist of the correspondence without scrolling down. If you want to e-mail a memo, send it as an attachment. (If you're concerned about the computer viruses that can plague attachments, paste the memo to the main e-mail text, but keep the introductory message brief.) Recipients can easily print out the memo to read. Long reports are better delivered in person or by messenger, or sent Express. If you absolutely must e-mail a report, attach it and apologize for sending such a lengthy report by e-mail.

Problem: Not replying to e-mails in a timely manner

Solution: All e-mails should receive a reply within a reasonable time. Some high-tech businesses thrive on quick solutions, so replies may be expected within 24 hours. In other types of more traditional workplaces, a bit more research and reflection may be appreciated. The point is to reply as soon as appropriate and reasonably possible and not leave the e-mail unacknowledged for a week or two. If a substantive answer is not quickly possible, reply within 24 to 48 hours that you are looking into obtaining the information and then try to follow up within the next 72 hours.

E-mails from colleagues should be responded to sooner rather than later. If you do not know the answer to an e-mail question, it is easy enough to press your Reply button and inform the sender that you will find the answer within a week. If you don't want to deal with a particular person via e-mail, respond to the message in some other way. Maybe ask your administrative assistant to call, which is a better alternative than ignoring the correspondence.

Conversely, don't be the type of self-centered and disorganized correspondent who always demands an immediate answer—flagging everything as important by using those urgent symbols—but then advises others that you require advance notice.

If you will be away for any length of time and have an Out of the Office Assistant software feature, set up an Auto Answer on your computer to alert senders that you will be unavailable and will not be retrieving messages until you return.

Problem: Failing to update the subject line and forwarding extraneous messages that are no longer relevant to the original subject

Solution: Always update the subject line (and always identify a subject to begin an original e-mail) when responding to an e-mail so that the recipient won't inadvertently delete your message. When you are replying to a single e-mail, include the original message; people answer many e-mails in a day and may not remember what they originally said. If you are sending the latest e-mail in a chain correspondence and the information in past messages is no longer relevant, delete it. You would be better off writing a brief summary that recaps what has been said to date and inserting a new subject line. Delete attachments that no longer are relevant as well so your recipient does not have to open attachment upon attachment. People are fearful of e-mail viruses and hesitant to unnecessarily open attachments anyway.

Problem: Absence of an e-mail salutation

Solution: It only takes a second to start with a salutation such as "Dear Iva" or "Greetings Leo" and it makes all the difference in the world. Recipients feel that you have recognized their existence. Closing with an ending such as "Regards" not only shows class, but ends with a positive (and lasting, as any successful salesperson will tell you) impression. This will serve you well in the long run.

Remember to say "please" and "thank you." Soften abrupt sounding demands ("Let me have it by 5 EST." with "Would you please send it by 5 EST?").

Problem: Flaming and sending e-mail bombs to others via an e-mail

Solution: Flaming is when a sender makes abusive attacks on someone else in an e-mail. An e-mail bomb is a comment irrelevant to the discussion at hand, such as on abortion or gun control, that is designed to provoke angry responses. In either case, do not waste time responding to such messages. The Web conference host should remove the submitter or warn of consequences. If the message is sent from one person to another at work, make a copy and take it to Human Resources or the sender's supervisor.

Problem: Typing in all caps

Solution: Most folks are not aware that this is tantamount to shouting at someone in netiquette (and can be interpreted as flaming). If you want to emphasize something by putting it in caps, tell your recipient that you are not intending to shout, but are only emphasizing. Otherwise, avoid typing in caps.

Problem: Inappropriate use of shorthand e-mail

Solution: Be discriminating when using acronyms, abbreviations, or other e-mail shorthand. This is just as important as using good grammar and spelling correctly (always remember to run the document through spell-check before sending it). You might feel comfortable using an e-mail shorthand to frequent interoffice correspondents. Refrain from this type of informality when corresponding with clients or e-mailing internationally.

!@!%#!@!%#!@!%#!@!%#!@!%#!@!%#!@!%#!@!%#!@!%#!@!%#!@!%#!@!%#!@!

Some Common E-mail Acronyms to Be Used Judiciously

BCNU—be seeing you
BTW—by the way
FWIW—for what it's worth
IIRC—if I recall correctly
IMHO—in my humble opinion
ROTFL—rolling on the floor laughing
TTFN—ta ta for now
TTYL—talk to you later
LOL—laughing out loud
HTH—happy to help or hope that helps
TIA—thanks in advance

Problem: Accounting for time and cultural differences when e-mailing across borders

Solution: Learn to be patient. Not only will the difference in time zones affect the time it takes to receive a reply (and don't forget that there are different time zones within the borders of many other countries, just as there are in the United States), but cultural differences will as well. People overseas are generally not so quick to respond to e-mail as those in the United States. If you ask them why, they would reply that they have better things to do than just stay plugged in. If you must have an answer immediately, telephone during business hours in the country you are calling.

Always include the time zone in your domestic e-mail. Do not say, "Please may I have this by 5 PM?" Say instead that you would like it by 5 PM PST. When e-mailing abroad, it often is easier to use date rather than specific time deadlines. (If you do need to refer to a specific time, remember to use the 24-hour clock; it is 17:00, not 5 PM.)

Also, be aware of public holidays in other countries; bank holidays and religious holidays are quite prevalent overseas, so that may delay replies.

Problem: Sounding parochial when e-mailing overseas

Solution: If you find that you are doing a lot of business with a client abroad, learn all you can about the country's culture, values, and beliefs. Try not to be ethnocentric and not to marvel at how much the client knows about your culture, which is not the center of the universe!

Avoid slang, which is rarely universal, and abbreviations, which are difficult to understand. Remember that seasonal references are not universal, either; your spring is someone else's autumn. And sports metaphors are never easy to understand. Never use "emoticons"—those facial expressions have different meanings in other cultures.

I advise employees of international companies to spell out dates to avoid confusion and be legally correct. In the United States, 6/12/01 is June 12, 2001, but to a German it means December 6, 2001.

Problem: E-mail viruses

Solution: While writing this book, my computer was infected by a virus that sent some of the chapters to randomly selected people around the world! (Please see Chapter 1 for a discussion of this vicious and uncivilized behavior.)

Yes, I opened an e-mail from someone I was not too sure about. The name rang a bell, but the message just didn't sound right to be from this gentleman. It turned out that a virus had hit his address book and randomly selected me as a recipient. I opened the attachment and encountered lengthy, complicated problems, which one does not need when writing on a deadline.

Try to be more alert than I was and never open an attachment that you are unsure of, even if it is your team leader sending it to you. I learned from this experience that it is safer to copy and paste your attachments in the text of the e-mail because viruses are sent in attachments; it really takes only a minute longer.

If you think that a virus has invaded your computer, be sure to notify the people in your e-mail address book by phone or from an uninfected computer. Warning them ahead of time is not only considerate but also the mark of a gracious colleague and friend.

Problem: Digital depression

Solution: Yes, digital depression. The symptoms of this new phenomenon are being constantly plugged in, unable to unplug long enough to type your reports or go talk to colleagues at work, and unable to relax with family or friends once you have left the office. Some people cannot focus on a task without checking e-mail every five minutes! Another sign of digital depression is when you fret that your latest gizmo is a dinosaur as soon as you purchase it.

Those who suffer from this technomalady must learn to schedule unplugged times to ensure a fulfilling life beyond work. Turn off your gadgets and take up a musical instrument, gardening, cooking, or another language. When you are no longer alive, you will not be remembered for being instantly available, 24 hours a day, 7 days a week. Go look for another job if 24/7 is what is expected in your organization. It is not a healthy life for you or a family. At times, all of us need to be plugged in, but not for 365 days a year!

MEETINGS
They're Supposed to Serve a Purpose

Meetings are the target of frequent jokes in the work world. And not surprisingly, for they are usually thoughtlessly organized and poorly run. When was the last time you heard anyone complain about not spending enough of his workday in meetings? After her harrowing commute and early morning exposure to incomprehensible voice mail and rude e-mails, the beleaguered worker in the vignette that opened this chapter probably had to go into a disorganized and sloppily chaired office meeting—ensuring that she would be thoroughly stressed out and on edge by lunchtime!

The logistics of successful meetings can be daunting. Frequently, the organizer has little expertise in actually running a meeting and keeping it on track. Attendees go into the meeting without knowing what to expect or what is expected of them. And everyone quickly gets frustrated and testy.

Here we focus on overall meeting etiquette, civil behaviors common to all types of meetings, including traditional face-to-face meetings or technomeetings, sometimes called virtual meetings, including teleconferences, videoconferences, and Web conferences, as well as training sessions (which may be either type), with a special emphasis on how to chair a meeting in ways that will raise expectations and enable effectiveness. When planning a virtual meeting, be courteous and sensitive to others' time zones. Take time differences into consideration so that one site does not always miss out on lunch or their family time in the evening.

Chairing a Meeting
You're in the Driver's Seat

Problem: No clear purpose

Solution: Most meetings fail because the chair has no sense of what she wants to get out of the session. If you haven't thought it through, why waste everyone's time? Face-to-face meetings are a rich source of discourse and interaction; they allow for eye contact and body language, which is missing from most other forms of communication, that provide valuable clues about interest, intent, and identity.

If you will be chairing a meeting, clarify its objectives at the outset and share this information with everyone who will be participating. Think about how the meeting can meet these aims and what ground you need to cover to get there. If your team leader has asked you to plan the meeting, ask her to explain clearly and concisely what she wants to accomplish through it.

Meetings can generate tons of questions, comments, and exchanges. The discussion that will ensue is useful if the chair knows how to move things along and keep the meeting focused on accomplishing its aims. Be aware that distracting side trips can occur. Attendees may seize the opportunity to move their own personal agendas forward. Think of chairing the meeting as navigating an obstacle course—you need to keep the end of the course in sight and concentrate on getting there.

Problem: Lack of agenda

Solution: Not having one will only bring chaos. People like to look good in meetings and will come prepared if you provide the information they need to do so. Distribute a meeting agenda to all participants at least two days and up to a week in advance. The agenda should spell out the topics to be addressed, make assignments of areas that individuals should be prepared to cover, and estimate the amount of time allotted for each agenda item, including a start and end time. Include a list of participants so that people know who will be in attendance. Provide thorough contact information for yourself as organizer, so that participants can clarify particulars with you well in advance.

Problem: No seating plan

Solution: A seating plan is not typically needed at internal meetings, where people usually know their places. At more formal meetings with clients, boards, committees, or vendors, a game plan is often called for. Observe hierarchy and assign the most significant participants the key seats. Place cards or name tents are often helpful and allow attendees to seat themselves. You might also ask your administrative assistant to greet participants and escort them to their seats with the aid of a seating chart, or assume this responsibility yourself if it is a smaller meeting.

Problem: Starting late, allowing interruptions, and generally not valuing participants' time

Solution: As chair, it is your responsibility to run a tight ship. Make it clear when you distribute the agenda that the meeting will start promptly as scheduled and that punctuality is expected. And calling a meeting for 10 AM rather than for first thing in the morning provides commuters less excuses for tardiness!

Start the meeting only about five minutes after it is scheduled, whether all participants are there or not. Request that attendees turn off their phones and beepers. Make it clear that none of the agenda items will be repeated. Thus, individuals who leave the room to check e-mail or voice mail, like latecomers, will miss critical discussion and will not be able to participate in the consensus that emerges. Let people know that you expect them to stay for the entire meeting; if someone absolutely has to depart early, he should inform you ahead of time.

By keeping the meeting on track, you demonstrate that you value participants' time, and they will respect you for that. On the other hand, people who earn a reputation for starting meetings late and running them loosely find that chaos prevails down the road when they schedule more.

Employees like to know in advance what their boundaries are. If you have never run meetings with precision, start to do so now by gradually introducing these changes and letting your staff know what you expect in the future.

Problem: Not following procedure

Solution: Procedural disputes can get ugly and are easily prevented by following commonly accepted rules of procedure. Chairs should familiarize themselves ahead of time with Robert's Rules of Order (universally accepted procedures for running meetings) and firmly but politely follow the procedures as outlined; this is standard meeting protocol. Even informal meetings should have some ground rules established at the outset regarding the format for discussion, turn for talking, and process for decision making.

Problem: Confusing brainstorming sessions with agenda-driven meetings

Solution: In true brainstorming sessions, all ideas offered are considered in no order of preference. The chair or a facilitator leads a discussion during which the best ideas surface. Everyone has a chance for input. It is a great process—but a very specialized one and not what one should expect when participating in a meeting with a clearly identified agenda and goal that are no longer in sight! If you allow this to happen, you are wasting everyone's time and courting chaos and discord.

When you want input for a meeting you are to chair, e-mail participants ahead of time soliciting their ideas and then select some of these items for the agenda. If you really want to brainstorm, say so up front and give attendees a feel for some of the issues you want to examine in the session.

Problem: People who talk too much

Solution: Nothing can dampen the collective spirit of a meeting more quickly than someone who drones on and on. A good chair will institute and enforce a three- to five-minute time limit on all speakers other than those presenting major reports that, determined ahead of time, require more time. Some speakers will take less time, others use their allotted minutes, no one monopolizes the floor, and the meeting moves along at a nice pace. Participants really appreciate this procedure.

Time limits also help with gender differences. Men tend to provide the nuts and bolts of an issue briefly, while women are more detailed-oriented and can take longer to cover a topic. This way everyone has equal floor time, and no one gets frustrated.

Some reports need to be longer than others—new agenda items, new business, a new committee, and so forth. The chair should have recognized this and provided these speakers with more time. If you are presenting such a report and have not been afforded adequate time, ask for more time ahead of the meeting; don't just presume that you can exceed your limit.

Proper Meeting Decorum
Everyone's Responsibility

Problem: Inappropriately eating at meetings

Solution: Don't bring your own breakfast or lunch to a meeting unless it has been announced as an informal brown-bag session. If breakfast is provided before an early meeting, it is typically served in a separate room, as is a luncheon during midday break. If pastries or bagels are offered with coffee in advance of a morning meeting, finish your snack before the meeting begins. If you are late, do without breakfast.

There's nothing ruder and more distracting than spreading your meal out, noisily unwrapping items, smacking your lips, and crunching away—unless everyone else is doing the same thing. Follow the lead of the chair. While sipping various beverages is permissible in meetings, dining in front of others who are not is juvenile and only demonstrates that your attention is focused on something other than the agenda.

Problem: Inappropriate personal activities

Solution: Carrying on some sort of grooming ritual, such as clipping or filing your nails, is inappropriate anywhere but in the rest room or in a private office behind closed doors. At a meeting, such behavior is particularly rude and irritating. Stop it!

Problem: Disrespectful behavior

Solution: Expressing disapproval of another participant or disdain for an idea is unprofessional, disrespectful, and rude. Facial expressions that show you disapprove can include making eye contact in a knowing way that says, "The speaker is a fool." Rolling your eyes or smirking are unacceptable as well, as are elbowing a colleague or kicking someone under the table. Remember that body language is interpreted differently in different cultures; shaking your head sideways in India, for example, indicates agreement rather than disagreement.

If you think someone is stupid, keep it to yourself. (If you open your mouth, you will only show yourself behaving stupidly!) Beware of trashing the meeting in conversation afterwards as well. What may seem like a silly thought to you today might be deemed a terrific idea tomorrow!

Problem: Shouting and carrying on

Solution: Displays of anger are counterproductive and should not be allowed for they only upset people and derail the meeting. If someone starts shouting and banging on the table during a meeting, the chair should calmly inform the individual that this behavior will not be tolerated. If the chair is behaving this way, meet with him privately at some point after the meeting and express your opinion that this type of behavior does not accomplish much. I did this once to a client who was a chair. My lucrative contract was not renewed, but his job did not last much longer, either. In fact, the department that he was hired to create and grow was eliminated altogether!

Teleconferencing
Somebody Still Has to Run the Show

Problem: Not having someone at the helm

!@!%#!@!%#!@!%#!@!%#!@!%#!@!%#!@!%#!@!%#!@!%#!@!%#!@!%#!@!%#!@!

Questions to Ask Yourself for Planning a Successful Meeting

1. Have I thought through what I want to accomplish in the meeting and set goals and objectives?

2. Have I solicited input about possible agenda items in advance if I want it—so that the meeting will not veer off course into a free-floating brainstorming session?

3. Have I put together and distributed to all participants an agenda that spells out topics to be addressed, assigns areas that individuals should be prepared to cover, and allocates time for each item on the agenda?

4. Have I set the meeting to start at an hour that allows participants adequate commuting time—and little excuse for being late?

5. Have I worked out a seating plan (unless it will be an informal internal meeting)?

6. Have I familiarized myself with Robert's Rules of Order?

7. Have I prepared my game plan for dealing with latecomers and "comers and goers," keeping the meeting organized and on track, eliminating disturbances by cell phones and beepers, and preventing disrespectful or disruptive behavior? And have I communicated these expectations to attendees?

8. Have I set time limits for speakers, allowing more time for those presentations that will require it?

9. Have I made it clear what the arrangements for meals will be?

!@!%#!@!%#!@!%#!@!%#!@!%#!@!%#!@!%#!@!%#!@!%#!@!%#!@!%#!@!%#!@!

Continued

10. If the meeting is to be a teleconference, have I let participants know how long it will last and how fully latecomers
will be allowed to participate? Am I prepared to identify participants at the onset and again if people join in late, and to
make sure that speakers identify themselves at the start of
each comment if there are a number of participants? Have I
arranged for a business interpreter if there will be overseas
participants?

11. If the meeting is to be a videoconference, have I stage-man-
aged the set to put the organization's best corporate foot
forward? If it is to be the company's first videoconference
with clients, have I held a mock conference so that our team
knows what is appropriate dress, posture, facial expression,
body language, and behavior on camera? Have I coached
them to wait a couple of seconds before replying to another
participant?

12. If the meeting is a Web conference, have I spelled out the
protocol to avoid flaming and e-mail bombs?

13. If the meeting will be a training session, have I communicated the value of the offering to the staff and given tips on
how employees can plan their day to accommodate the
course?

Solution: The participants in a teleconference may be scat-
tered around the country or around the world, but it's still a meeting. The biggest problems will still arise from lack of a steady
guiding hand, which results in a teleconference that is disorganized, confusing, and adrift.

Whoever calls the teleconference is in charge and should set
the agenda and establish the guidelines. You owe these courte-
sies to the others who will be involved. Let the participants know
in a memo or e-mail how long the teleconference will last and

what the policy will be toward latecomers. Mention that everyone's input is valued, so it is important that everyone joins in at the appointed time. If the conference starts to veer off course, you as the organizer should bring it back into focus.

Problem: Participants who do not keep to the appointed time

Solution: It is extremely frustrating and disruptive when someone joins in late and then asks for points previously discussed to be repeated or attempts to change decisions already reached. This is highly unacceptable behavior.

If you are more than a few minutes late joining in (20 minutes, for example), call, apologize, and ask permission to participate. Assume that you have missed some essential points of discussion—this is your own fault—and move on without asking people to repeat themselves or trying to influence previous business. It is, however, acceptable and desirable to ask that those on the line reintroduce themselves. If you are an hour late (this can happen because of flight delays and such), ask if your input is absolutely essential and what it is that people need to know from you.

Take responsibility for scheduling travel realistically to accommodate teleconference schedules and try your best to arrange to be somewhere where you can join the conference on time and without difficulties. Take responsibility for clarifying time differences in different parts of the country or of the world. You know that flights are always delayed and that delays will continue to worsen. Plan accordingly and don't schedule a teleconference for 20 minutes after your scheduled arrival time. In other words, do not make everyone suffer to repeat everything because of your own poor scheduling skills.

Problem: Not following proper conferencing protocol

Solution: Politeness and deference are even more important in a teleconference than in a face-to-face meeting to avoid total confusion. Identify yourself each time you speak if there are more than five or six participants; this helps compensate for the lack of visual identification. Always permit other speakers to finish what they are saying before replying. Don't cut in; it's not only rude, but disorienting as to who is speaking.

Problem: Assuming everyone speaks your language

Solution: English speakers are quite arrogant in making such an assumption. If you are teleconferencing with people overseas, have a business interpreter (not a translator) in the room with you. Even if your overseas counterparts speak English, they may occasionally lapse into using their own language when they confer with one other. Your interpreter will be able to pick up on the nuances of the negotiations and report them to you later. Let your counterparts know up front that you have an interpreter in the room with you, should anyone need this service.

Videoconferencing
You're on Candid Camera

Problem: Failure to prepare for the medium

Solution: I advise organizations to stage a mock meeting when they are about to videoconference for the first time. It is a good way to familiarize yourselves with the medium, which is growing by leaps and bounds thanks to the increasing complications and costs of air travel. Because the trends are toward multisites around the globe and outsourcing, teams are spread out; one of the easiest ways to bring them together is via videoconference. However, first-time use of this meeting forum is fraught with peril, particularly if you are videoconferencing with clients. You could easily mouth something disparaging and get caught, for example. There goes the account! Tell your participants that a videoconference is not to be watched passively. They are not on a couch at home! They should come professionally prepared to make contributions.

Problem: Inappropriate posture, presentation, or behavior

Solution: This type of behavior shows that you are not paying attention. Clean up your act; you're on TV, after all. The camera has a roving eye and will catch you scratching your nose while gazing at the ceiling in utter boredom, making faces or vulgar gestures, doodling pornographically, or talking to each other. Big mistake. Just because you are not sharing the same physical space does not mean that you are at liberty to misbehave. Even if you cannot see everyone else, assume they can all see you. (If you try to check e-mail on your laptop on the sly, the camera's roving eye will likely catch you.)

Dress for an on-camera appearance. Pay attention to posture, sit properly, and act in command of yourself and your surroundings. Try to look relaxed and smile occasionally. Be aware of body language and facial expressions. If you yawn, cover your mouth. If you itch, scratch discreetly.

Bear in mind that there is a voice delay in a videoconference and take special care not to interrupt. Be patient and wait for a couple of seconds after someone has finished speaking before taking your turn. This is especially important when some of the participants are overseas.

Also, as with all technology, things can go wrong. This is not a magical black box! Remain calm, if this happens. A professional technician will have a sign saying, "We are experiencing technical difficulties" come up on the screen. Keep your composure and refrain from bad mouthing the technical people.

Problem: Eating and drinking during a videoconference

Solution: Unwrapping, crunching, and other eating sounds are magnified and even more unpleasant in virtual meetings. In videoconferences, the noise may trigger a signal switch causing the camera to rotate automatically, putting you on-screen with a mouthful of food. This will make you look unsightly and cause the person who was originally speaking to lose focus and become upset.

Problem: Uncivilized accoutrements on the meeting table

Solution: Having a sea of Styrofoam cups on the table beside you depicts a lack of class, and writing with cheap throwaway pens on a bunch of dog-eared pads projects a less-than-upscale image. Pay attention to stage-managing the videoconference, especially if you are conducting business overseas. It absolutely bewilders many people in other cultures how we U.S. Americans, the richest people on earth, seem to surround ourselves with so much junk.

This is an opportunity to use that expensive pen your aunt gave you at graduation and that handsome leather portfolio you received for doing some thankless job. Make a point of bringing along a real glass to drink water from or a nice china cup and saucer for your coffee or tea. And use real spoons, not those plastic stirrers!

You don't have to bring out the bone china and sterling, but pay attention to detail and make sure the meeting room is presentable. Artwork and photos on walls, as well as plants, are recommended as backdrops for this medium so that people will focus on you, the speaker, and not on the blank walls or bare room. If this is an overseas account, hang diverse art.

Use name tent cards with large lettering that is readable through the monitor. If you are videoed in your own office, tidy up the desk so that you look in control of your workload and your professional life. All this will portray your organization in a good light and present an image that says that these people care about quality and likely offer quality goods and/or services.

Problem: No one directing the show

Solution: Once again, proceedings will begin to flounder if there is no in-control chair making introductions, advancing an agenda, and otherwise connecting the dots to complete a successful meeting scenario. If you are running the conference, try to include all participants on video and do not relegate some to telephone contact only. If someone's image is not on the screen, he or she will not be fully engaged by the other participants. If this is impossible because of a lack of technology or budget reasons, make sure that the people on the phone are constantly brought into the discussion.

If participants have not been adequately introduced, try to compensate when it is your turn to speak. Ask who is in charge and suggest that everyone identify themselves and what they do. If you sense that the meeting is beginning to derail, ask a question designed to steer things back on track when you have the opportunity.

Web Conferencing
The Web Grows More Tangled

Problem: Rushing to embrace the new technology without adequate thought and planning

Solution: Web conferencing is gaining more and more attention because of economic cutbacks and nervousness about flying in the wake of terrorist attacks. While this form of meeting by typing on the Internet is indeed an inexpensive way to bring your virtual team together, it is also fraught with perils. Silicon Valley workers may be at home with Web conferencing, but those in more mainstream industries still face a daunting learning curve. Before opting to rely heavily on the technology, consider the following factors:

- Web conferencing is recognized as the cheapest and quickest way to hold a meeting. However, does that necessarily equate with quality? One engineering firm told me that they prefer to combine teleconferencing with Web conferencing because cheapness is not the image they wish to convey. (They also believe that if a face-to-face conference is not possible, hearing voices at least makes the dialogue somewhat personable.) This firm uses the Web component to display slides and have their people preview written presentations that participants can then discuss later in the teleconference.

- Web conferencing is more conducive to an informal culture. (Once participants start chatting on an open page, it can become a free-for-all with everyone from your team not necessarily on the same page.) If you are meeting with clients who have a more formal culture and an established hierarchy, consider a different medium—especially if they are overseas and not from a high-tech industry!

- Virtual teams sometimes meet on the Web over a three- or four-day period with people fleeting in and out, going to sleep and then reentering the meeting. These can get discordant and become unmanageable.

Problem: Choosing Web conferencing technology without taking participants' needs into consideration

Solution: It is inadvisable to select this medium only because it is available, becoming popular, and you can do it! Ask yourself the following questions:

- If your team is multigenerational, does everyone have the same typing skills? You may find that younger workers raised on the Internet are able to keep up with the flow of typed conversation, while others are left behind. This is irksome to many people, who will become frustrated and edgy.

- Is anyone on your team dyslexic or physically disabled and unable to type?

- If some members of your global team have to type in a second business language, are they going to be able to make valuable contributions as speedily as the rest? These people are more adept with the verbal language.

Problem: Choosing among the plethora of Web conferencing software systems

Solution: Evaluate and choose carefully. For example, do you really want a system that allows typing only in lowercase or only utilizes limited punctuation marks? (Where does a new sentence begin and end? When is a new thought beginning?) Once you have made an educated choice, get your whole team using the same software, so that you will all be dealing with the same issues as you progress through the learning curve.

Problem: The anonymity of Web conferencing that makes people feel they can be rude and careless

Solution: Establish clear guidelines in advance. At the start of a conference, you might suggest that everyone identify themselves, at least by their initials, before they type anything. Remember to keep to a thoughtful pace and write messages that are shorter than what you are reading. When the keys start flying, people can easily become careless in their thinking and writing. One of the benefits of a Web conference is that it can be recorded and archived to be viewed on demand—so warn people that their comments may be preserved for posterity! This helps maintain a civil meeting.

Training Sessions
Learning Should Be a Lifelong Process

Problem: Attendees with a negative attitude

Solution: Organizations schedule training to improve the bottom line by enhancing employees' skills and enabling them to reach their full potential. Some sponsor outstanding programs that are among the most important employee benefits offered.

Individuals should realize that unless they constantly advance their abilities, they will be out of work in today's fast-paced marketplace. Attend training sessions with an open mind, participate fully, and absorb as much as possible. If others are giving the instructor a hard time, try to get them to show some respect so that you can learn.

Problem: Not enough time for a training session

Solution: Make time. Trainers can often spot tomorrow's leaders—the stars are the ones who identify and go after the skills they need rather than waiting around for the course to be mandated. They self-manage. They are on the phone requesting courses that may not even exist yet.

Acquiring knowledge is never a waste of one's time. Your e-mail and voice mail will be there for you when you return to the office. Work a little later than usual that day if you need to catch up.

Problem: A facilitator who is not prepared

Solution: Unfortunately, everyone is not professional, and you may encounter this problem on occasion. Make do the best you can and immediately report the trainer to the Training or Human Resources department. (But make sure that the problem is genuinely with the facilitator and not your own.)

Problem: Implementing eLearning (training sessions on the computer) without fully considering the technological capabilities of end users

Solution: The creators of these programs need to carefully evaluate their audience's technological capacity and test early with a variety of employees to ensure acceptable capabilities. As too many organizations that have rushed unprepared into eLearning can attest, it is disastrous to design programs only for the fortunate few with the most "horsepower."

Problem: Not explaining the anytime/anywhere aspects of eLearning to employees

Solution: The realities of anytime/anywhere must be clearly conveyed to employees. You'll have a revolt on your hands if they interpret it to mean that they must pursue a mandated course online in their free time as they would elective MBA programs. Employees must be told that they may choose between having dedicated, uninterrupted time to do so during work hours or staying home to take the course. Offering incentives such as points toward a trip or prizes encourages employees to complete their courses.

Problem: Not taking individuals' different learning styles into consideration

Solution: Experts in the field such as Carole Wald (who can be reached at Carole@frontier-learning.com) note that the dropout rate for eLearning can be high if various learning styles are not accommodated.

Essentially, there are two eLearning methodologies: Synchronous eLearning allows for real-time interactions with instructors and other students online (Web conferencing) regardless of location. Asynchronous eLearning can be pursued anytime/anywhere without simultaneous participation.

Whoever designs the mix has to consider the DNA of the organization and the learning preferences of the employees. Sometimes both eLearning methodologies supplement actual class time, mentoring programs, face-to-face discussions, and reading/study groups. Communication with the instructor via e-mail is always helpful.

Poll your people and do not impose technology on them just because you can. Determine the most effective approach!

CONFERENCES, CONVENTIONS, TRADE SHOWS, AND EVENTS
Networking Opportunities Galore

Some employees find these pumped-up meetings and myriad special events energizing, while others see them as boring. I find that what you get out of them is pretty much determined by the attitude you bring to the general session, the exhibit floor, or the cocktail reception.

Networking is the most important function at these events, and you probably are wasting your time if you don't make the most of the prime opportunities to do so. Let's face it, the more relationships you nurture outside your own box, the faster you will accomplish business goals; you will build information resources that enable you to do your work in less time than the average performer.

Furthermore, these megameetings provide significant opportunities to get to know a number of your colleagues better and give them a chance to size you up. When the next opening comes up in one of their organizations, they might think of you!

There are, of course, problems to overcome and protocol to master regarding conventions and trade shows. Individuals are away from home and free of the daily shackles and supervision of their offices; the temptation may be to act out or goof off. Many individuals find themselves in a much more public position of spokesperson and goodwill ambassador for the organization than they are used to or initially comfortable with.

And then it takes nerve to work a crowd of strangers! Remember that you have to give to get. Open up—tell people what you need and ask them how you can be helpful. Always make plans to stay in touch. With a few guidelines, most people can mingle with ease.

Problem: Not introducing yourself

Solution: Remember that the other person probably feels as intimidated as you do, and that introducing yourself doesn't entail a major commitment. Just go up to the person, read her name tag (which should be placed on your right side so that someone shaking your hand has a good line of vision), and say, "Hello, my name is Roger."

If someone doesn't want to talk to you or demeans you, move on. It is their loss, not yours.

For in-house events, find out who the senior officers of the organization are and approach them so they have an opportunity to get to know you. Remember that your words convey only about 7 percent of the message, your tone and inflection about 38 percent, and your body language 55 percent.

If you stay with your friends, you are not networking. Any salesperson will tell you that is the wrong approach. Try to learn more about conference issues and exchange information and ideas with the people you meet; it can be an enriching experience. Odds are you will feel much better about mingling once you have engaged two or three people in conversation and swapped business cards with them. And do not avoid people who are different from you!

Problem: People who engage in flirtatious behavior

Solution: You do run into one of these jerks occasionally at conventions and trade shows. They have clearly misinterpreted the meeting's raison d'être and are in the wrong place. Move on quickly and leave them to wallow in their egoism.

Problem: Bad-mouthing your own organization

Solution: I learned this as a diplomat: No matter how disgusted you are with your government's policy, you still represent that government. The same holds true with a business. You represent the organization, which issues your paycheck, pure and simple. Your words and actions should demonstrate this. Never put down the organization or say anything cynical in public, no matter how negative the news has been or how painfully your CEO may have stonewalled on the witness stand. Respond to disparaging remarks with some appropriate variation of "The matter is under litigation, and it will be interesting to see how it unfolds!" You can always try to diffuse the situation by turning it around and showing interest in the businesses, work, and products of questioners.

If you want to show sympathy for someone else whose organization has been suffering from bad press or plummeting stock, just say, "Things must be difficult for you right now." This leaves it up to the individual to determine how much he wants to talk about the situation. Don't gloat. Remember, if another's house is on fire today, yours might be tomorrow!

Problem: Booth representatives at trade shows who spend their time talking to each another and ignore visitors

Solution: This is a major problem. People with little experience may be hired to work trade shows and then dispatched to the exhibit floor with little training. Attitude can prevail. If you notice such behavior by your booth colleagues, try to facilitate more interaction with the public and less internal chitchat among them.

If you are a visitor, gently but purposefully interrupt the trade show reps who are too busy with their conversation to acknowledge you and ask you what you need. They should at least greet everyone cheerfully and chat briefly before attempting to determine whether someone is a serious prospect or not. Conversely, browsers who do not have any serious interest in ordering should not take up too much of their time.

Problem: Overcrowded booths

Solution: Crowd control is crucial. Booths should be designed to allow the free flow of movement around circular tables for taking orders and conducting other business. If a booth is getting crowded, a representative might move his conversation into the aisle. Another representative could be posted at the entrance to request that visitors come by later or wait until space clears up.

Problem: Representatives who treat the booth as a lunchroom or a break room

Solution: Keep your booth neat and uncluttered. It is not professional to spread food out in a booth and eat your lunch instead of assisting customers. (A beverage is acceptable, but please substitute a nice glass or cup for those ugly cardboard containers and hide aluminum cans.)

Arrangements should be made to have relief personnel fill in during meal or rest breaks. Sitting (not sprawling) to rest is permissible if the booth is empty, but as soon as a visitor walks in, one should stand up and pay attention to that potential customer. Even if the booth is empty, don't sit with your hands behind your head and legs spread out in front of you. Maybe that is why the booth is empty—you are chasing away people with your body language.

Problem: Getting obnoxiously drunk at a special event

Solution: If you have a drinking problem, never drink alcohol at business functions. Nothing will ruin your reputation and chances for a promotion faster than this type of degrading behavior, and you will be avoided like the plague. Do not do anything out of the office that you would not do back in the office.

Problem: Not replying promptly to invitations for events and receptions and not keeping commitments to attend

Solution: This huge problem can wreak havoc on meeting planners and hosts. All I can say is that class tells! Please do not make your hosts call you repeatedly for an answer.

As soon as you receive an invitation, check your calendar, block out the time in your planner if you are going to attend, and reply promptly (RSVP). No one will think that you are too eager. If you need to coordinate with a spouse or guest, call immediately and nudge for an answer. If you reply in the affirmative, it is your duty to show up. If you decline, do not decide to show up at the last minute. If you travel a lot, arrange for your assistant or the neighbor who takes in your mail to look out for invitations so you can respond in a timely fashion.

Problem: Determining how to thank folks for events and receptions

Solution: Sometimes, just popping your head into a meeting planner's office and mentioning what a pleasant evening you had is sufficient. At other times, more formal acknowledgment is called for. If the CEO of the organization invited you to dinner, for example, send a handwritten note afterwards. Remember that it can feel lonely at the top and reciprocate the invitation—it's a great opportunity to show off your culinary and entertaining skills, which are all about how well you organize!

Certainly all luncheons and dinners should be acknowledged either by a handwritten note or a phone call depending on the circumstances. If folks invite you to sit at their table at a fundraiser, acknowledge their kindness in a note. Even if it is a company table, they took the time to put the group together and should be thanked for including you.

BEYOND THE BOX
Behaving Outside Your Own Space

We don't live in our offices or cubicles—nor in meetings, the dynamics of which were examined in previous pages. We leave our "box" throughout the workday, headed toward various destinations within the organization for any number of business or personal reasons. On the way, we're bound to run into many of our colleagues, and how we interact with them in these encounters reflects on our professionalism. Let's take a look at some of the day-to-day interactions with coworkers that can cause problems, from simple greetings to health concerns, profanity to hostile behaviors.

Introductions and Greetings
Good Cheer Can Be Infectious!

Problem: People not reciprocating your greetings in the hallway or elevator

Solution: We all crave acknowledgment. We want to have a sense of belonging. Keep it up and people will begin to respond. Give them the benefit of the doubt that they are preoccupied and not purposefully rebuffing your greetings.

Always say "Hello" or "Good morning" or "Good afternoon" as you encounter coworkers on your rounds. And, of course, respond in kind if they initiate the exchange. If you run into someone to whom you have never been introduced, stop and introduce yourself. Sometimes, especially in the southern United States, Hawaii, or Puerto Rico, people linger a while for a chat. Far from disrupting the business at hand, the brief exchange of pleasantries provides a wonderful break, helps you get to know and appreciate your colleagues, and spreads good cheer!

Problem: Failure to introduce people to one another in any business situation

Solution: This is a common occurrence; all too often one is left to introduce oneself. If no one introduces you and you are left to stand there, jump in and introduce yourself: "I am Yasmin Kahn, the Vice President of Marketing. How do you do."

Try to get in the habit of taking the lead and introducing people to one another. Business etiquette books address the subtleties of introduction protocol, but I believe that as long as you make the introductions, the hierarchies really don't matter. The goal is to ensure that people get to know one another. I suspect that most people neglect introductions because they are so afraid of getting it wrong. Just go ahead and make your introduction instead of fretting. Leave the protocol intricacies to the diplomats and folks at the State Department.

When making an introduction, always try to mention a job title or something that the parties might have in common. If you can't think of any common interests, add something about the workplace. Introduce a junior accountant named Adam Smith to Maria Rodriguez, an editor from a client's firm, by saying, "Maria, I would like you to meet Adam Smith who is an accountant at our firm. Adam, Maria Rodriguez is an editor from the XYZ account. You both lived in Nicaragua in the 1980s."

Problem: Improper use of titles

Solution: Governor, Judge, Mayor, Doctor, President, Professor, and Senator are titles to be used frequently. Even former ambassadors are addressed by their title. If you have a problem with using titles, get over it. You are not demeaning yourself by addressing someone correctly; quite the contrary, you show sophistication. When making introductions, use the title as well.

Problem: Improperly addressing someone by their first name upon introduction

Solution: Never assume that you can use first names. Wait until you are given permission, or ask if you may call people by their first names. Sometimes, people will object to such informality. At other times, it might make someone more comfortable. An employee in the mailroom might be embarrassed by your using her last name, for example, so ask if you may use her first name. "How do you do, Ms. Clark. May I call you Susan?" will suffice.

Problem: Forgetting names of people you have just met

Solution: This is a very human occurrence, I am afraid, even with civility gurus! Repeating a name when you first hear it can be useful, as can using the name in the conversation that ensues. Sometimes, it is beneficial to think of an association in your mind, although you have to be careful—if the association you make with the name is humorous, you may inadvertently end up treating the person in a funny way!

Never, under any circumstances, disparage someone's name. Doing so only demonstrates how unsophisticated you are. I have often been made fun of because of my name, which makes me feel very small and hurt. Just because my name is unusual, that does not entitle you to laugh at it or at me. When I find a name difficult, such as a Chinese name, I hold the person's hand with both of my hands, focus intently on them, and have them repeat it for me. If they say, "Call me Jo," I say, "I prefer to call you by your Chinese name. Please give me a minute to master it." Names are part of people's identity and respecting them shows concern for an individual's sense of pride. And you shouldn't give someone a nickname right away—even if you are the president of the United States! It is offensive and can make you come off as a clown.

Problem: Improper response to an introduction

Solution: This is simple. In business settings, just say "How do you do." Save more casual responses such as "Nice to meet you" for informal social occasions.

"How do you do." is just a polite phrase for acknowledging an introduction, not a question that requires an answer. When the other person says, "How do you do." don't answer "I am fine, thank you. How are you?" Often, two people will say "How do you do" at the same time and segue into a conversation.

Problem: Not shaking hands

Solution: Once you get used to shaking hands, it won't feel so awkward. Simply look a person in the eye, grip his or her right hand firmly with your own, and shake a couple of times. Hold your shoulder back and look confident.

Shaking hands is often an appropriate gesture when you are introduced, arrive for a business meeting, close a deal, or leave an event. Remember always to stand up for an introductory or farewell handshake. And, yes, businesswomen should stand as well.

At functions, hold your drink in your left hand to always keep your right hand free for handshaking. If your hands are full, excuse yourself from shaking at that moment; if you are introduced to a person whose hands are full, do not extend your own hand. Be thoughtful!

Problem: How and when to exchange business cards

Solution: Always have an adequate supply of business cards ready in a pocket for presentation as soon as the oral introductions have been made and everyone is comfortably seated. (Give people time to settle down before whipping them out.)

When you receive someone's card, read the information on it—don't just glance at the card and put it away. If on reading the card you realize that you did not introduce a person correctly, take the opportunity to make amends, "I apologize. I did not realize that you are the Senior Vice President. I introduced you as the Vice President."

Some Westerners go to ridiculous lengths trying to present and receive cards in the traditional manner when doing business with the Japanese. Unless you have lived and worked in Japan, this is not necessary. You are a Westerner, not Japanese, and it is sufficient for you to show respect by reading the card.

Life Events
Caring Response Is Appropriate

Problem: Determining who to invite from the office to a wedding

Solution: Usually a direct supervisor should be invited out of courtesy, along with close friends at work. As a coworker, you should not expect to be invited, for the betrothed is not obligated to invite your whole unit or all other coworkers. Don't get into a snit because you weren't invited. There are so many limitations—such as type of ceremony and reception, budget, family considerations, and who is paying and therefore entitled to invite more people.

Those invited should buy gifts individually. If the entire unit is invited, then a collective gift from the unit is appropriate. Sometimes the betrothed will host a separate party for colleagues, or coworkers might want to give the betrothed a bridal shower. This is not an obligation, unless you are a tightly knit group. Individual or collective gifts are appropriate under these circumstances.

Problem: Proper acknowledgment of the birth or adoption of a child into a coworker's family

Solution: If you are close to the coworker, a birth acknowledgment is a gesture of goodwill. A personal gift for the parent or the child is suitable, and some offer of assistance—with shopping or cleaning, perhaps, while the new parents have their hands full— will always be appreciated. A baby shower before the birth is an appropriate option if you are close, but it is not an obligation.

Problem: Death of a colleague or of a partner or relative of a coworker

Solution: When a colleague passes on, the family should make the necessary arrangements, depending on how they want to remember their beloved. Every "family" (remember, not all surviving significant others are relatives these days, but might be an unmarried or gay partner or a close friend) handles death in its own way, which must be respected. Some will recognize that coworkers might like to pay tribute to a deceased colleague, while others will want to grieve in private. Be particularly solicitous of a coworker who has lost a life partner, whether married or living together (straight or gay). Treat the loss of an unmarried partner the same as you would that of a husband or wife.

After someone has died, offer your immediate verbal condolences to your coworker or to the survivors and ask what you can do. Then wait at least two or three weeks before sending a handwritten note or letter, which is preferable to a card. The note should say something about how kind or helpful the deceased was to you and offer assistance. (Waiting allows the survivors time to handle arrangements for services and all the paperwork associated with illness and death.) Do not consider sending flowers as necessarily taking care of your obligation. (Check about the survivors' wishes; not everyone wants flowers. And flowers sent at a later date may remind the bereaved of the funeral and cause quite the opposite of your desired effect. Some request that contributions be sent to favorite charities.)

Many people appreciate a visit, an offer of assistance, or an invitation to dinner. The Jewish custom of sitting shivah for seven days, during which time family and friends visit the bereaved, is a wonderfully supportive tradition.

After some time has passed, such as a month, the organization might want to hold a memorial/celebration gathering for the employees, to which the deceased's family and friends can be invited. It is a nice gesture to present an album with stories about the workers' relationships with their late colleague and maybe photos taken at work of old friends together during happier times.

Whatever you do, do not just forget about the loss and treat the bereaved colleague or the survivors of a coworker as though everything were all right. It is not. Many who have experienced a loss will need your support four to six months later; be there for them.

The CEO and supervisor should keep in touch with the survivor, ensuring that all paperwork, health benefits, pensions, and so forth are transferred without hassles. Remember the survivor during the holidays and keep in touch on a regular basis. One person who was splendid at this was President Lyndon Johnson. After President John Kennedy's death, President Johnson was always phoning Jacqueline Kennedy and inquiring as to how she was holding up. If such busy people have the time, so do we!

Problem: What to do about the death of a coworker's beloved pet

Solution: Be there to offer comfort and advice. For many, the loss of a pet is just as significant as that of a relative.

Health Concerns
Employ an Ounce of Prevention

Problem: People who cough, sneeze, or yawn without covering their mouths

Solution: The solution to these health hazards is so simple—cover your mouth. Politely remind coworkers to cover their mouths, if they forget, so that they don't infect others through droplet exposure. And gently remind them that we really do not need to see their latest dental work!

Problem: Failure to wash hands after using the rest room

Solution: People forget to wash their hands all too often. Putting up a notice in all rest rooms—reminding people to wash their hands and under their fingernails—can help stop the spread of germs. A written notice tends to jog one's memory.

Problem: Touching body parts at work

Solution: Mostly a male thing! If you must scratch, tug, or pull at an appendage, do it in a bathroom stall. Then wash your hands. This behavior can spread germs and just plain grosses out others.

Profanity
Clean Up Your Act

Problem: Expletives in the business environment

Solution: How much is acceptable? The answer is easy. None. Swearing makes you appear unintelligent and in command of only a limited vocabulary. People focus on the expletive, rather than the substance of an argument or presentation. Blasphemous expressions and racial slurs make you come across as uneducated and small-minded, which will drive away business. Putting bad words in writing is even worse—they remain in the record forever and give a reader the impression of crudeness. Nor are vulgar hand gestures acceptable.

Problem: Swearing as part of the culture at a workplace

Solution: Unfortunately, there are businesses where profanity is de rigueur. Car dealerships, law firms, construction companies, and some high-tech industries come to mind. The existing culture in such organizations will not change overnight, and an individual who tries to change it will be "mobbed" (see page 120). A new leader has to come in and institute slow reform.

Choose where you work wisely. There are thousands of workplaces where swearing is not condoned (even some construction crews and law firms), because it reflects poorly on people, products, and services. If you're stuck for now, try to work it out with colleagues by asking them not to cuss in front of you. Of course, if you are a client, you may always request that profanity in any form not be used in your presence.

Hostile Behavior
Do Unto Others . . .

Problem: Criticizing and blaming

Solution: If you are a supervisor, you are undoubtedly mindful of the rampant blame culture. "It's not my fault" has become the plaintive whine of the early 21st-century workplace. It is known as the "attribution theory" in the social sciences. People blame others for their errors and then try to make themselves look better by unnecessarily criticizing the ability of their coworkers. It's all such a waste of time. Ask employees to focus on their own work and to do an honest appraisal of what has gone wrong. Personal responsibility is a concept that has been out of favor for too long and needs to be firmly reintroduced into the workplace.

Problem: Rumors/gossip/backbiting

Solution: Often spread out of jealousy, innuendo creates a malicious work environment. Some experts advise listening to the rumor mill to stay in the loop, but I think it's best to steer clear. My approach is to tell the rumormonger that I do not want to hear it—and that I would hope that were she to hear any gossip about me, she would clarify the matter with me personally before spreading it around.

Nothing can pollute the atmosphere of an office faster than rumor. When I worked for the Seychelles government, the rumors were often vicious and destructive. Most were lies. As an international consultant, I find that employees try to pull me into their intrigue and make me take sides. My solution is to work off-site as much as possible and never, ever get involved!

A friend once sent me an e-mail that you might want to keep in mind: "Great minds discuss ideas/Average minds discuss events/Small minds discuss people." (Author unknown.)

While I was writing this book, two rabbis formed an organization with a Web site, <www.wordscanheal.org>. They have launched a national multimedia ad campaign aimed at getting U.S. Americans of all ages to pledge to show more civility in their talk and deeds. That means no gossip, no backbiting, and, unless you really cannot help it, no unkind words toward your fellow humans. I suggest that we all go to this Web site, take the pledge, and think more about the words we use and about how what we say can hurt other people.

Problem: Violating trust

Solution: Don't do it. It takes years for someone to learn to trust you, yet that trust can be broken in seconds. Hold people's confidences close to your heart, even if you feel that they have betrayed you in some fashion. You may need them again someday!

Being mindful of your obligations at work is preserving the circle of trust. Be reliable—show up on time, do what you are supposed to do as well as you can, and hand in reports when they are expected. Remember to keep your appointments, phone back when you say you will, and look into matters that colleagues are relying on you to. If you tell someone, "Consider it done," follow through on that commitment. Your word should be your bond. When there are unreliable people in an organization, it weakens the interdependent structure. That is why employees sometimes fly off the handle—there is always someone not keeping the faith. Being faithful to your responsibilities is a mark of professionalism.

Problem: "Humorous" put-downs

Solutions: Many people try to put down others in the guise of humor. In fact, the most hostile person in the organization may be the office clown. This is unacceptable behavior; the joke is still a put-down. If she says, "What's the matter, can't you take a joke?" reply, "That was not a joke. It was a personal attack leveled against me. You would not like it if the tables were turned. Please do not repeat it." If she says you are too sensitive, say, "It is easy to level that accusation when the 'joke' is not on you."

Problem: Derogatory remarks

Solution: As soon as someone makes a remark to put down you or someone else, say, "I do not appreciate being spoken to in this manner" or " I think a little more sensitivity is called for here. Please do not talk like this when I am around."

Often ethnocentric, sexist, or racist in origin, derogatory remarks can be horribly hurtful and destructive to individuals, teams, and organizations. The worst such remark I have heard in the United States was about how someone had just swum across the border and "his back was still wet." I took offense and told the person who made such a low comment, "We all bring our own talents, energy, and contributions—whether we came here on the *Mayflower,* arrived by plane, or swam."

If you are the victim of a personal attack, try to turn the tables on the aggressor. If someone makes a derogatory remark about the university degree you obtained overseas, as if to say only a U.S. university degree is legitimate, just answer, "I would like to see you survive in a different system and get ahead. Education anywhere is beneficial. Maybe we can learn from each other." You will not hear another derogatory remark from that person.

A friend of mine was once told that she was not good with the computer because she was only a "coconut." (In Australia and New Zealand, "coconut" is a derisive term for a Pacific Islander.) At the time, she did not feel empowered to answer back, but after reading *Rude Awakenings,* she told me she would be prepared now! Or, maybe the boss who made this thoughtless remark would be more enlightened if he had read my book—and would not have said such a thing!

Problem: Yelling and screaming

Solution: No one has the right to behave this way. If someone yells and screams at you—anyone—do not take it. As soon as the tirade is over, say, "When you have calmed down, I will be happy to talk to you." And walk away. After a cooling-off period, tell the individual that it was unacceptable behavior and that you refuse to be treated that way again. Document the incident and report it to Human Resources or to your supervisor.

Problem: "Mobbing"

Solution: This is the term used to describe a situation in which coworkers gang up on and shun an individual. This hurtful and childish behavior is not uncommon. It still happens in many places, such as in union shops or among administrative assistants in some corporations, as well as in highly technical workplaces.

Mobbing may stem from any variety of reasons—the perpetrators believe that the victim is an informer, or that she did not go along with a majority decision. The causes can also be highly political. If the most powerful person in the organization is a

Republican, others follow suit. If you are a Socialist, you may be shunned, criticized, and driven out.

!@!%#!@!%#!@!%#!@!%#!@!%#!@!%#!@!%#!@!%#!@!%#!@!%#!@!%#!@!%#!@!

Working for a Jerk

No office is without at least one. Bullies who thrive on creating fear, they engage in various combinations of the hostile behaviors we're talking about—mobbing, criticizing the work and downplaying the accomplishments of others, threatening job loss if they're in the position to do so, yelling and screaming and fist pounding, swearing, making derogatory remarks, and making fun of people. Known in civility jargon as "instigators," these jerks can be peers, middle managers, or leaders.

If you work for a jerk, plan your strategy for a private dialogue with the individual. Explain that you do not like to be treated in this manner and describe the impact that his behavior has on you. Say, for example, "Screaming at me in front of other people makes me feel diminished, and I cannot produce effectively." Look him in the eye and talk politely about how you want to be treated. Tell him, for instance, that you do not want him to raise his voice or use profanity. Or that you would prefer that he use civil tones.

Try to leave the meeting with an agreement. If he has told you that your tardiness in everything frustrates him, tell him that you will try to be on time. You both should have your own goals to accomplish. You are showing courage, yet trying to help him save face. Often, you will stop a jerk dead in his tracks faster by talking to him directly.

Be aware that a jerk thrives on bullying those he perceives as vulnerable. (Research shows that single women are the biggest victims of this abuse, along with thinner women and people from different racial backgrounds, as well as the disabled.) If you cower, the jerk will win and you will be a wreck. If you show that you are mentally strong, this will neutralize his position.

!@!%#!@!%#!@!%#!@!%#!@!%#!@!%#!@!%#!@!%#!@!%#!@!%#!@!

Continued

The following day, greet the jerk nicely to show that no hard feelings exist. If you are chronically late, try to improve. If his behavior starts to change, praise him for it. If it does not, document every unacceptable behavior that ensues to ensure that you do not receive an unfair performance appraisal.

If the abuse should reoccur, tell the jerk that you are documenting the incident this time and that if the "hostile work environment" continues, you will pursue it further. Take this second incident to Human Resources and put them on notice about a "harassment" or "emotional distress" situation as warrants.

During my ambassadorship at the United Nations, there was a concerted effort by some delegates to isolate the Ambassador of Egypt with the silent treatment because of his government's rapprochement policy vis-à-vis Israel. U.S. diplomats not speaking to the Palestinian Liberation Organization (PLO) at the U.N. until the late 1980s was also unproductive. This is not what diplomacy or relationships are about, and it is best not to participate in behavior that is meant to coerce someone else.

Systematic intimidation of a targeted person in the workplace is emotional abuse and should not be tolerated. Report it to Human Resources, discuss it in your unit, or say something in an Employment Attitude Survey.

COMMON FACILITIES AND RESOURCES
Incivility at Its Worst

All the organizational development professionals and Human Resources directors who I spoke with identified this area as the greatest source of incivility and tension in the workplace. One can only imagine what kind of homes some people must come from!

Common-area problems range from the merely frustrating, such as copy machines nobody seems to have the time to fill with paper or doors not held open for coworkers loaded down with files, to the truly disgusting and dangerous, such as trashing women's rest rooms (by women, I might add) in what seems to be some sort of passive-aggressive protest.

Senior management officers have told me in interviews that they feel embarrassed to have to even raise some of these issues. Dealing with them takes vital time away from work and customer needs, but the problems have to be addressed nonetheless.

Problem: Not holding doors open for others

Solution: Believe it or not, this is one of the most vocalized complaints in the workplace! It is insulting to people when you slam doors in their faces—even worse when you fail to hold the door open for someone whose arms are full. There is no senior hierarchy or gender difference here, just common courtesy. Whoever gets to the door first holds it open, especially if the person behind is loaded down. And you always hold the door open for a client, male or female.

Help other people, for heaven's sake! If they don't thank you nicely, they are uncivilized. (I know people who innocently say "You're welcome" when someone fails to thank them for holding a door open, which usually elicits a belated and somewhat sheepish "Thank you.")

Problem: Employees who rush to get in an elevator—and then refuse to step to the back

Solution: This behavior is extremely annoying and causes office congestion, as well as irritation. When these employees rush to get in as soon as the elevator doors open, others who want to get out on the floor have to struggle to do so. When people headed to the top floor refuse to step back, they make everyone else elbow their way around and out.

It's time to make these people behave like grown-ups. Put notices in the elevator reminding coworkers of elevator manners, or include the reminders in a booklet. Don't remain silent; speak up at employee meetings about how frustrating this is.

Problem: People who stand all over the place on an escalator and block others from passing

Solution: To ensure efficient movement and courtesy, please stand on the right (in the United States, on the left in some countries) and allow room on the left for those who want to pass. Bunching up and talking to friends causes congestion and raised tempers.

!@!%#!@!%#!@!%#!@!%#!@!%#!@!%#!@!%#!@!%#!@!%#!@!%#!@!%#!@!%#!@!

Eight Actions Sure to Alienate Coworkers and Disrupt the Office

1. Let doors slam in the faces of coworkers, especially when they're weighted down with files or equipment.

2. Charge into an elevator before letting anyone else out.

3. Refuse to move to the back of the elevator, even when you're going to the top floor.

4. Stroll away leaving a copier or fax machine that's run out of paper without refilling it or telling anyone, or a nearly empty coffeepot ready to burn.

5. Use the watercooler for any purpose other than for what it was intended (such as brushing your teeth).

6. Trash the rest room.

7. Leave smelly food containers, dirty dishes, and debris stacked in the kitchen or common area.

8. Steal food from the office refrigerator.

Problem: Workers who pilfer supplies from the storeroom

Solution: Let it be known that this won't be tolerated. A few pencils here, a stapler there—and maybe a couple of legal pads and some envelopes—may not seem like much, especially if you work for a huge corporation. But a huge corporation has thousands of employees, and the losses can add up pretty quickly if many of those employees help themselves to supplies. How would you feel if your cleaning lady felt equally entitled to the pick of your household goods?

Problem: Not refilling paper when copy and fax machines run out

Solution: This sounds like a minor irritation, but it is the source of a lot of kicking and banging and cussing. Just watch the traffic at a busy office copier some time. The machine always seems to be out of paper when people are most in a hurry. No one seems to know how to fill it. And no one seems to be available to help. Asking employees to be individually responsible on this issue is a losing battle. It shouldn't be, but it is! You know the expression, "Choose your battles." This is one battle I readily concede and I find that paying an administrative assistant extra to be responsible solves the problem instantly. He makes sure paper is readily available for the valiant few who refill for themselves, puts his name and extension above the machines to be contacted when refills are needed, and then usually checks the paper supply periodically so that he never receives a call.

Problem: Employees who misuse watercoolers

Solution: I personally witnessed one employee brushing his teeth at the office watercooler (which usually elicits a chuckle when I recount the story, but on further reflection is no laughing matter) and another at a different organization spitting into it! There are major health concerns here. Do not assume that this type of gross behavior doesn't occur at your workplace.

Watercoolers are generously provided to employees for quenching their thirst. They also make good places for coworkers to gather and spread some good cheer. Brushing one's teeth at the cooler or spitting into it spreads diseases and is unsightly. It's unfair to other employees who use it. The best solution is to educate people about the potential health hazards and remind them of the proper use of a watercooler.

Problem: Filthy women's rest rooms

Solution: There is a new phenomenon occurring in women's bathrooms all across the corporate United States, which involves leaving soiled feminine hygiene products lying on the floor, not wiping urine from toilet seats, and flushing paper towels down the toilet or littering them around the sinks. (The men's bathrooms are cleaner, it would seem.)

While some Human Resources personnel I interviewed see this as a consequence of absent parents and poor hygiene training, others interpret this terrible behavior as a "passive-aggressive" protest against unpopular female bosses. Evidently, there is always a correlation between a filthy bathroom and proximity to some notoriously mean-spirited female manager.

Not only does this create significant health hazards, it also punishes other female employees, not just the boss. A two-layer solution is to put notices in the stalls about proper hygiene and to let employees know at unit meetings that there are other ways to deal with bully bosses. If an organization dumbs down about this issue and labels those who complain about the mess as "too fussy," they will lose good employees.

The in thing right now is for organizations to reintroduce "fainting rooms" equipped with lounge chairs, soft music, magazines, and sometimes even aromatherapy in women's rest rooms—places of rest and relaxation where employees find refuge from the fast-paced world of ringing phones, e-mails, and noisy cubicles. You can imagine how disturbing it would be to find filth and debris here, and managers can threaten to take away this privilege if the bathrooms continue to be messy.

Problem: Dirty and messy lunchrooms and recreation rooms

Solution: An organization does not have to provide employees with break rooms. If a problem develops with napkins littered all over the floor, dirty plates stacked in a corner, and stale food in pizza boxes and takeout containers piled up on the table, I say just lock it up. Management should tell employees that the Board of Health would not tolerate it, and neither will you! After one company did lock the lunchroom doors for a month, the staff began to pay more attention to cleaning up after themselves. If management takes the issue seriously and shows employees that to be treated like an adult you have to behave like one, behavior will improve.

Problem: Stealing food from the office refrigerator

Solution: This seems to be one of the most common of workplace dilemmas, even at high-end corporations. Some Human Resources managers have told me that it is another "passive-aggressive" reaction, meaning if your food is constantly stolen, someone is getting back at you. But blaming the victim doesn't address the problem. Moreover, this kind of offense is a bully's tactic to subvert the organization, because it affects the whole company—not just one or two people.

I think that many people are simply too lazy or cheap to stock the refrigerator with their own food; stealing is a much easier alternative. Once again, values at home may not have been properly reinforced, and some people are just incorrigible. Managers should threaten dismissal if anyone is caught stealing food. Discuss it as a serious problem at unit and organization-wide meetings. Choosing to belittle the problem or ignore it will only lower morale and productivity.

Problem: Smoking in prohibited places

Solution: In the United States, state and local laws largely regulate smoking in the workplace. Most workplaces today are smoke-free environments. Smoking is an established health hazard, and it is unfair and disrespectful to violate this prohibition by, for example, sneaking a cigarette in the bathroom.

Some workplaces have a designated smoking room that is well ventilated and set aside for smokers. This enables people to enter the building without having to pass through an omnipresent cloud of smoke generated by the smokers assembled outside the front door. It also makes smokers feel as if their needs are being taken into consideration, instead of their being banished.

Some organizations encourage employees not to smoke while representing them off-site as well. (It is especially important to try to adhere to this rule if you work for a health-related organization!) International visitors are often unaware of our smoking regulations, so please inform them politely of our rules.

MODERN OFFICE SETUP—MOSTLY CUBICLES
The Plot Thickens

Problem: Lack of forethought in designing office layouts

Solution: The goal of using cubicles was supposed to be to foster open communication and creativity. Personally, I think it is just cheaper for an employer to pack people in so tightly. All cubicles do is fuel rage—especially if the transformation to cubicles is not accompanied by civility training. I know of organizations that pay people modestly but put everyone in their own offices, including administrative assistants. That is something to think about in terms of a better quality of work life.

If you must use cubicles, put all the sales staff, who routinely make lots of phone calls, at the opposite end of the room from engineers and others who need to work quietly. Install cubicles with higher walls—at least 64 inches, with fabric material to cushion sound.

Problem: People with private offices not observing cubicle protocol

Solution: Those who have private offices should be glad they do and be mindful that people working in these oppressive cubicles do not have much privacy. Loud social chats in one cubicle disturb people in the neighboring cubicles, for example, so speak softly when you go visiting. If you just want to ask a quick question, an appointment isn't necessary. But if your meeting is going to take more than 30 minutes, call and make an appointment with a cubicle occupant. He has work to do, too!

Be respectful of others' time and deadlines. Not having a door does not equate with an open-door policy. Some companies that I have worked with have tried employing cues such as asking cubicle occupants to wear specifically colored caps when they do not want to be disturbed. This solution, however, is unpopular with many women because of the "hair issue." Putting orange tape across the entryway to let others know that someone needs quiet time has generated better results, but only if everyone in the organization knows what the tape means—and complies.

Problem: Cubicle dwellers not observing cubicle protocol

Solution: Respect yourself and your neighbors. Yelling over a cubicle wall to someone in a distant cubicle to ask a question is disruptive to many. Everyone pops up their heads to see what's going on (known as "prairie dogging") and this is very annoying.

There is no acoustical privacy in this type of "open plan," so talking in a loud voice to a visiting colleague or over the phone is unfair to the person next door. Moderate your voice and limit your use of speakerphones when conducting meetings or listening to voice mail. Use headsets.Try to make personal calls at lunch; people do listen, you know! Keep your radio and music volume to a minimum, preferably listening through earphones. Profanity should not be allowed. Because there is no ceiling directly above your cubicle, the airspace is public!

With all these invisible boundaries in mind, request a conference room if you plan to hold a lengthy meeting or a speakerphone conversation. Remember as well that computer screen
savers must reflect a business image and that items posted in
your cubicle, such as banners, photographs, and posters, must
also be professional and not offensive. In the final analysis, this is
"your" space while at work, but ultimately it still belongs to the
employer. Try to avoid clutter and maintain an organized space
appropriate for business.

Eating in a cubicle might cause problems, depending on how
much odor your food emits. Going to the lunchroom is more considerate under some circumstances. Take a document with you if
you must work during your lunch break; others in the room will
understand.

If you share a cubicle (horrors), grant your cubicle partner
equal space. Keep all of your plants and photos on your side.
Don't set plants on top of the cubicle wall, where the person next
door has to contend with your creepers; no matter how pretty you
think they are, this is invading your neighbor's space.

Problem: Abused cubicle protocol

Solution: If you have a problem with a neighboring cubicle
resident, go have a friendly chat. Be pleasant about the situation;
the person is probably totally unaware of the problem. And if you
receive a complaint from a neighbor, don't fly off the handle.
Accept it politely and tell the complainant that you will see what
you can do to make things better. Apologize—that usually amelio-
rates tension fast—then do something to correct the situation.

If a problem persists, document it for your supervisor. If it is
treated lightly, say that you are taking it to Human Resources. A
loud radio or swearing next to you is not only unpleasant, it
diminishes your productivity. I have had to intervene in thousands of these situations, usually because management took an
initial reported incident lightly or treated it with scorn, permit-
ting the problem to escalate out of control.

Problem: Regularly using office machinery without tailoring it to the needs of the individual or providing proper support systems (Using devices such as computer keyboards and cash-register scanners can lead to repetitive-motion injury, which costs business billions of dollars in turnovers and absenteeism.)

Solution: This is a simple respect issue that recognizes that physical pain can occur while using certain office equipment. Most administrative assistants and cashiers still lack the clout and empathy they need to get help and relief, but some high-tech organizations have become more sensitive to this type of problem.

SAS, a software company, has created personalized workspaces that meet the needs for work efficiency and comfort. They provide all kinds of adjustable machinery and furniture to accommodate their employee needs.

RELATIONSHIPS WITH CUSTOMERS/ MANAGERS/COLLEAGUES
We're All in This Together

We touch here upon some of the more serious relationship issues in the workplace. If employees are not comfortable in their dealings with the organization's customers, with senior management and leaders, and with each other—to say nothing of the organizational culture and milieu—you've got problems.

I start with the customers, for they are often the most ignored segment of the business world. In researching business etiquette books and other resources, I noted with perplexed curiosity that dealing with customers was a topic almost never addressed. And in my own consulting work, I am often called in to solve problems among coworkers, but seldom have I been told that innovations were needed to impress customers, despite the fact that Impression Management is a growing field to which more businesses should pay attention.

Customers
Often Given Short Shrift

Problem: Lack of sensitivity toward customer needs

Solution: It never ceases to amaze me how cavalier employees can be toward customers. Their phone calls go unanswered. They are not listened to attentively. Their queries are treated with scorn. They are mocked and put down behind their backs! The customer, whether external or internal, is the profit center—remember that. You, the employee, are overhead.

Learn to anticipate your customers' needs, values, and cultural makeup. Survey them on a regular basis. Purposefully, but respectfully, advise them on your areas of professional expertise. You do not have to bulldoze your knowledge, but this is the time to strut your stuff. Tell them when you disagree and back up your recommendations with facts.

Remember that it is much easier and cheaper to keep customers than to win new ones. Make life sweet for them. Keep in touch by sending newspaper clippings of interest, congratulatory notes if you have read or heard good news about them, and letters of condolence when they are mourning. Defer to them when they talk about their hobbies or interests. Open doors for them.

Some executives send flowers on customers' birthdays. Others invite good customers to their VIP suites at sports events. Some companies send gifts during the holidays. For clients abroad, find out about their holidays and send them something special. A Hindu customer will be pleasantly surprised that you knew about Diwali and took the time to acknowledge it! Your bottom line can only grow from such consideration.

Senior Management
Get with the Program

Problem: Managers who don't manage

Solution: Southwest Airlines "hires for attitude and trains for skills," but most organizations promote star producers into senior management because of their technical abilities. It can be difficult to transition from producing to managing, even more so when you have to demonstrate expertise in both areas. Often, no one bothers to address new managers' people-managing abilities (or lack thereof) or provide them the resources they need to develop these skills.

When you accept a management position, be prepared to be fair and to liaise equally with a variety of people. Make yourself available and listen to everyone with due respect. That is why you are being paid the big bucks. Abdicating your role as a solution finder for employees with problems is gross negligence. A manager who treats a complainant with derision, or belittles her issue, is courting disaster. If the company does not offer you the people training you need, demand it. It is difficult to be an executive—try to live up to the role.

I have to mention a trait of many managers I observe, which is sometimes referred to as "promoting mediocrity." Many people in positions of power are so insecure about their own aptitudes and abilities that they surround themselves with relatively incompetent employees. This enables them to browbeat the staff while feeling superior. How many of us have actually been told that we were overqualified for a job? What does that really mean? Excellent managers who don't worry about their own level of competency hire the best people they can find and are thrilled for the quality help.

Interactions with the Leader
Remember Who Signs the Paycheck

Problem: Treating the leader as an adversary

Solution: Some people are averse to authority and automatically assume that a leader is the enemy. With a good relationship, however, a leader will help you grow professionally. With a positive attitude, you will move up the ladder faster.

Work amicably with your leader. Whether you are setting performance goals, going through appraisal reviews, or discussing strategy, treat your boss with respect. In most cases, leaders have more experience than you do. Accept criticism and do not automatically assume that it is unfair.

If you receive a review in which your work is pegged as substandard, the best approach is to take a deep breath and inquire about what you can do to improve. A leader would be doing you an injustice if she did not discuss your weaknesses and help you find solutions. Try to map out an action plan together for improvement, including extra training or a coach if needed. Carrying on with swear words is counterproductive, as is placing the blame elsewhere unless the review really is off base. An honest, on-the-mark performance review is a rare gift.

Problem: Asking for a raise

Solution: Timing is everything. If economic times are bad, large raises are not going to be given. If a company has had a bad fiscal year, you are unlikely to receive a huge raise even if you are a star.

During times like these, you might want to look to nonmonetary benefits to make up for the large raise you are not going to get. Think about such benefits as club memberships, airport limousine rides, day care, dry cleaning, access to a company resort facility, or an increase in your life insurance. Good things come to people who ask. But you must know how to ask and how to negotiate, which means that you win some and lose some. It's give and take, not just "I want, I want. . . ."

During better economic times, when raises are ripe for the picking, the best approach is to build a solid case and have industry standards at your fingertips. Point out the profits that your department generated and how much this contributed to the growth of the organization, then show how you factored directly in this growth. Sometimes growth is measured in other ways—how many new members you recruited, the good publicity you orchestrated, and so forth.

Do not tell your leader that you need a raise because you want to buy a new car or because you have maxed out on your credit card. You will rightly be shown the door!

Remember that your personal evaluation is key to getting the raise, which is why it is good to learn how to handle criticism. Those who take direction well get the thumbs-up for upward mobility! Believe me, I learned this the hard way. When you are young, you tend to be arrogant and think you have all the answers.

Interactions with Peers
We Are Family

Problem: Poor relationships with peers

Solution: Cooperative relationships with coworkers are crucial. They not only make the workday more pleasant and productive, but improve the quality of your life and let you sleep better at night!

Coming to work on time, following through on projects, pulling your weight, producing work that no one else has to finesse, and minding your own business are constructive behaviors that will help greatly in getting along with peers. If you're having problems with colleagues, do an honest self-appraisal. Analyze what it is about you that is causing conflict.

If someone else on your team typically exudes a sour personality, flies off the handle, and never wants to lend others a hand, find the courage to take this person to lunch and ask, as a friend trying to help out, if anything is the matter. These folks are often unaware that their personal unhappiness is causing others pain. (Sometimes the problem is even caused by a chemical imbalance that needs adjusting with medication.) Suggest counseling or going through the Employee Assistance Program. If this is too unpleasant a task to undertake, ask the supervisor to do it.

Problem: Team projects that always seem to end in bickering

Solution: We tend to be individualistic in the United States, and teamwork can be very challenging for us. Teams need a clear leader who makes people feel that they are welcome and have a sense of belonging. Using project management software is not project management. If the project is a huge and lengthy one, bring in a project management consultant to help get you started.

At the onset, set procedures, informal rules, and norms, especially how disagreements will be solved. Sort out the strengths and weaknesses of each member and assign tasks accordingly. If one team member is good at researching and another is an excellent writer, the division of labor should make the most of these skills. Utilize project management techniques, such as scoping, that include discussions on quality work, target completion, and budget guidelines.

Begin your project with the end in mind. Establish the objectives clearly at the beginning and emphasize that relationships are important and that interpersonal performance will be evaluated along with skills. Talk about people's work habits. When you set timetables, initiate discussion on how some people thrive on deadlines, while others clearly do not. Talk about finding a happy medium, about time organization, and about the importance of team members not always demanding things as soon as possible from each other. Nothing should be left unsaid; most teams end up bickering, because we dive in without discussing things.

Adjourning a team brings it to closure. The project leader should have a get-together and express appreciation. Recognize everyone's efforts and be aware that if you have had a well-functioning team there is going to be a shared sense of loss over the suspension of activity.

Problem: Lack of sensitivity to colleagues with disabilities

Solution: Most companies state that they do not discriminate against people with disabilities. However, how many visibly disabled people do you encounter in the workplace? Disability can still be a new phenomenon to many individuals. That is why it is important to have a unit meeting when you hire someone with a visible physical challenge. Prepare coworkers before prejudice has a chance to set in.

Be fair. Treat people with disabilities with an attitude of appreciating their abilities.

- The majority of us have some form of disability, many of which are invisible (just ask the millions of men who use Viagra). Some people are dyslexic or have attention deficit disorder and have developed coping skills to manage. Some have language disabilities and cannot acquire a second language. Others are clueless when it comes to a sense of direction. None of us are in a position to make light of the disabilities of others. Nor should we stare or do anything else to draw attention to those with more visible disabilities. Emphasize people's strengths rather than their disabilities.

- Learn to feel comfortable among people whose disabilities may be more obvious. Include them in your teams in professional and social activities. Be prepared to travel with them to off-site meetings. Engage them at meetings and don't act as though they are pariahs. Even if they appear awkward while performing a task, let them do it themselves unless they ask for assistance. Offer handshakes to the disabled. People in wheelchairs want to be acknowledged with handshakes. You might want to ask a blind person, "How do you do. May I shake your hand?"

- Do not become uptight and too politically correct in the presence of disabled people. If you say to a wheelchair-bound colleague, "Let us walk over to a restaurant for lunch today," she will not take offense. On the contrary, she will be grateful to be included. I have a blind friend who always asks me to describe things in detail when I tell her that I wished she could "see" a painting or a piece of jewelry. This is just a regular conversation between friends and I do not treat her differently from my "seeing" friends.

- Face a hearing-impaired person while speaking to him, for he may understand by lip reading. Don't yell—the person may have partial hearing. Don't be distracted by the presence of an interpreter if there is one, who is signing and/or speaking; focus your attention on the deaf person, rather than on the signer.

Listening
It's Amazing What You'll Learn

Problem: Not listening well

Solution: I once heard a presentation from one of those business gurus who said that to be a good leader or coworker, you had to learn to "listen generously." How true! Although I teach better listening skills in my civility workshop, I myself struggle constantly with honing my own listening abilities. Growing up, I was taught that to be a great communicator, you had to be a good talker. But as I grow older, I have come to realize that listening is just as important!

Listening well helps us gather information essential to navigating work and life, yet failing to do so is one of the most common flaws. The good news is that we all can change our bad habits and become better listeners. First, we have to choose to start listening carefully, not to "half listen." I find that if I make eye contact, focus intently on the person who is talking, and nod my head occasionally, I listen better. I am connected to the speaker.

Influential and powerful people use this skill all the time. They may be the center of attention in the room, but when they are talking to you individually, they take in every word and make you feel as though only you count at the moment. Try it. At a networking event, instead of looking over someone's shoulder to find out who else is in the room, focus on the person who is speaking to you and "listen generously."

In order to listen, you have to be prepared to hear. If you are reading e-mails while on the phone, you are not fully listening. If you are daydreaming about your hot date while the leader is explaining a work assignment, you are not fully listening. If you are thinking about what to say next during someone else's presentation at a board meeting, you are not fully listening.

Like a Zen Buddhist, be in the moment at meetings. Take deep breaths and listen to others carefully with an open mind. Let yourself be curious about the speaker: Listen to vocal tones, observe gestures, and try to connect with a nod or a smile. And take notes, so when it is your turn to speak, you can incorporate a few references to previous presentations. People will be greatly impressed.

Keep in mind that there are three types of listening. Combative listening is the way we listen when we are more interested in promoting our own viewpoints or in looking for a weak point in the other party's position to rebut. This is not "listening generously" but rather "listening internally." Passive listening is what we do when we assume we have heard everything, without verifying any of it. This is only half listening.

On the other hand, active listening involves not only hearing what someone is saying in terms of words, but paying attention to feelings as well. We may not agree, but we are trying to understand from the other person's perspective. When we listen actively, we employ a demeanor of respect. We do not smile when someone is expressing sadness. We paraphrase what we have heard and send back verification. Sometimes called "listening externally," this is "generous listening," or what I would call "superior listening."

Occasionally, you need to combine your listening skills. A lawyer, for example, might employ combative listening in a courtroom and active listening with a client. Remember that most of us are able to fully listen, we just must learn to do so.

Negotiation
It's Amazing What You'll Gain

Problem: Too much focus on negative external factors

Solution: Our political system in the United States is based on a winner-takes-all approach that we tend to carry over into other aspects of our lives. In business, we need to adopt a less adversarial win-win approach and convey that attitude to those with whom we are negotiating.

Stop wasting time studying the opponent's modus operandi, digging up dirt, looking for ways to "screw" the other guy, and offering ultimatums. All this expends so much negative energy needlessly. If you do not know what the other side wants, ask. Learn to defer: "You know this business better than I do. What would be fair?" Start treating the other side as the other party, not as the enemy.

!@!%#!@!%#!@!%#!@!%#!@!%#!@!%#!@!%#!@!%#!@!%#!@!%#!@!%#!@!

Questions to Ask Yourself Before Entering Negotiations

1. How do I behave in negotiations?

2. Is the process one I enjoy or simply loathe?

3. What sort of climate will I help create?

4. Will I put out friendly vibes—or ones that say "kill"?

5. Am I comfortable with moments of silence?

6. What body language am I using? Folded arms that indicate I am closed to suggestions?

7. Can I afford to walk away?

8. Am I going to have patience?

9. Do I want a quick deal, even at the expense of a long-term or potentially long-term relationship?

10. Will I try my best to listen externally and not to my own inner dialogue?

11. Am I comfortable with my own internal power level?

12. Will I help others get what they want so I get what I want?

Problem: Not focusing enough on our internal strengths

Solution: Your "internal power level" has to do with your degree of personal self-confidence and the authority with which you exude it. It is a strength you bring to the negotiating table that no one can diminish, no matter the importance of a title or the size of an organization. I learned this lesson in the diplomatic arena, where larger countries often try to use their external power to bully smaller countries. The smaller countries, however, often can rally internal strength that would leave the bullies utterly flabbergasted!

So even if you are a middle manager negotiating with a senior vice president, show some inner resolve. Just never let it come out in an arrogant fashion. Believe in your position, but be willing to compromise. Remember not to dig in—it's difficult to climb out of a hole!

Problem: Not listening well

Solution: No, this is not a repetition of our discussion of listening abilities, but a demonstration of the importance of that skill. In negotiations, we need to fully listen to what the other party is saying, rather than carry on an inner dialogue in preparation for combatively presenting our own next point. We need to learn how to listen to the message, not just the words. This will tell us what the other party really wants. Learn to listen well to begin to understand what his true interests are. Then be prepared to think two or three steps ahead, as you would in tennis or chess, and anticipate what will then be asked or answered!

Problem: Failing to follow up on what you have heard

Solution: Once you have discerned some of the other party's real interests, be prepared to give up something to accommodate them. This is conceding, not losing. It is a strategy that builds trust and confidence. Remember that you have to allow the other party to save face. Know what your acceptable settlement range is. You will not always walk away with everything you want, but achieving 60 percent to 75 percent of your objectives is a win as well! Negotiation is an art that involves compromise. If all you want is for the deal to go your way, then you are being unrealistic.

Global Negotiations
Globe Trotting Is Not Glamorous

Problem: Impatience with the negotiation process and failure to take the time to understand other cultures

Solution: For U.S. Americans, developing a patience quotient and appreciating how others negotiate is paramount to success in global negotiations. How they view time is essential to your knowledge. There is always the temptation to enter into negotiations overseas to get a fast deal. But winning for the short term and alienating people in the process is losing for the long term, because you have not created sustainability.

The corporations that are successful in the global area are the ones that have learned these lessons. A high-ranking representative from Sprint who I interviewed was emphatic about the importance of building long-term relationships overseas and engaging in win-win negotiations that lead to more deals. She expressed concern about the negative consequences of rapid deal making, stressing that you have to be fair and give people reasonable time frames in which to operate.

A representative from Shell echoed these sentiments and related a story about how it once took him six months to secure an agreement from a civil servant in Malaysia. After many office visits, much casual chat, and a series of chess games, a sufficient level of comfort had finally developed that enabled the civil servant to ask, "What can I do for you?"

Representatives of global organizations soon learn that international civility goes well beyond whether you kiss, bow, or shake hands. The French, for example, have a *non* ritual that is always the "primary refusal" in any negotiation—whether it is a marriage proposal, a request to sit at a particular table, a treaty, or an opening business offer. Many see this as rudeness and consider the French difficult. However, it is a ritual. The French would be disappointed were you to turn away and quit, because the *non* will become a *oui* in some fashion, eventually, if you persist. Not everyone is as direct as U.S. Americans. The Indians and Pakistanis can argue every detail. It gets exhausting, but you have to hang in there and be prepared to banter.

Problem: Not hiring appropriate people for international work

Solution: Both Shell and Sprint stressed that hiring the right talent is crucial. This is where most organizations make a mistake; they hire parochial people with technical skills who do not have the international experience needed for global work. You should hire those with the necessary international knowledge and experience and provide them with the technical training if that is possible. If you find candidates with both skills, you are truly fortunate. If they have technical training and you must absolutely hire them for overseas, then drill them for weeks on international skills. Do not just send them out into the world expecting that they will cope. They will likely lose the account for you!

Both the Shell and Sprint spokespersons noted the impact of civility training on customer acquisition and happiness, vendor relationships, and employee retention overseas. This included intercultural training and conference calls between in-country and offshore officials to discuss culture-specific history, traits, and negotiating style before entering a new overseas market. Tip lists from more experienced staff were shared.

Sometimes protocol/civility consultants were brought on board as well. International staff were required on an ongoing basis to take courses on negotiations, listening skills, ethics, accountability, and the manners of the country with which they would be working. Staff listened to outsiders brought in to relate stories and discuss challenges to prepare themselves for coping with similar situations.

Ethics
Would You Bet Your Job on It?

Problem: Lack of preparation for ethical quandaries

Solution: When I ask participants in my workshops, "What are ethics?", I am often shocked at how little they understand about the concept and appalled by their lack of interest. So many organizations fail to instill the notion of ethics into the corporate culture!

Sprint, the global communications company, has detailed policies about ethics and valuable educational material, including pages of sample questions and answers about possible ethical dilemmas. (See Sprint's Ethics Quick Test on page 145.) It is a fantastic tool for an employee, a wonderful preemptive instrument. No assumption is made that everyone understands the concept of ethics and would know how to deal with an issue if it came up. There is also an ethics help line, which employees can contact anonymously.

I particularly like Sprint's statement on the subject: "Sprint's reputation, and your conscience and good name, are far too valuable to do anything that wouldn't pass the Ethics Test. In a nutshell, this means that all of us must tell the truth and fulfill our promises. And we must treat all stakeholders—fellow employees, customers, suppliers, investors, and communities—with honesty, decency, and respect."

We all benefit from working with principles we believe in and with people who support the same value systems. Alan "Ace" Greenberg of Bear Stearns said in *Lessons from the Top: The 50 Most Successful Business Leaders in America—And What You Can Learn from Them,* by Thomas J. Neff and James M. Citrin (Doubleday, 2001): ". . . promote whistle-blowers. Ethics are everyone's responsibility. People who identify lapses and errors should be rewarded." Greenberg pays his employees 5 percent of the value of any error that they uncover; he has written checks for as much as $60,000. "You do not want to rely on an internal audit committee, where it takes years to find something," he warns.

!@!%#!@!%#!@!%#!@!%#!@!%#!@!%#!@!%#!@!%#!@!%#!@!%#!@!%#!@!

Sprint's Ethics Quick Test

Sprint values integrity, and wants to maintain its reputation for doing the right thing. If you're ever in a situation where the right thing is unclear or doing the right thing is difficult, examine your options with the Ethics Test:

- Could it harm Sprint's reputation?
- Is it ethical and legal?
- What would my family and friends say?
- How will it look in the newspaper?
- Would I bet my job on it?
- Should I check?
- How would my action appear to others?

Stress
The Organization Can Be the Cause or the Solution

Problem: Feeling irritated and under pressure

Solution: Try to defuse stress—and the negative behaviors it can precipitate—by taking in deep breaths or going for a walk, even if just around the block or down the hall to the watercooler. Focus on calming down.

To prevent stress in the long run, the most important steps are to exercise on a regular basis, always eat balanced meals, get enough sleep, and have annual checkups. Cut out fast foods and junk TV, and cultivate friendships and hobbies. Try to get massages, meditate, and, most important, have a life out of the workplace. Refuse to be plugged in on a 24/7 basis. The sun will come out tomorrow, and you will have another opportunity to do more work!

Look at the example of one sane U.S. corporation that makes huge profits but does not thrive on relentless pressure. At SAS Institute, which is probably the most important software company that you have never heard of, the employees eat lunch with their children, everyone gets unlimited sick days, and the gates clang shut at 6 PM for most of the employees. Furthermore, this is just a portion of a sound strategy to retain people by keeping them productive, healthy, and relatively stress-free.

In a world of signing bonuses and stock options, this is a place where loyalty matters more than money. SAS does not offer monetary incentives to come to work for them. They have been around for a long time, and they have lost only about 5 percent of their employees per year during boom times when jobs were plentiful everywhere in the industry.

SAS has a massive fitness center and programs that help their employees "de-stress," including massages and classes in African dance, golf, tennis, and tai chi. They even provide laundry service for employees' sweaty gym clothes to encourage them to keep using the gym!

If you are an SAS employee, it is virtually impossible not to be able to do your work! If you are worried about finding assisted living for elderly parents anywhere in the country, you can call the company's elder-care coordinator for assistance. If you're concerned about what to do with youngsters, don't be; child care is available on the premises. And there's no need to juggle doctors' office hours and deadlines, just go to the on-site clinic for your allergy shots. No wonder this organization is always on someone's top list as a good company to work for in most categories. Money is not everything—sanity is!

RECEIVING VISITORS AT THE WORKPLACE
A Little Forethought Goes a Long Way

While a few companies appoint a Director of Protocol to handle the logistics and finessing of receiving visitors, particularly international dignitaries and high-level executives, most, sadly, do not. Only about 1 percent of U.S. corporations give this business imperative the attention it deserves. And when a CEO goes overseas for the first time, he is embarrassed by the lavish attention imparted from the moment he arrives until his departure.

In our increasingly competitive and global economy, it's important to take the time to manage first impressions and put your best corporate foot forward before getting down to pitching the product, closing the sale, or negotiating the contract.

Problem: Ill-prepared and inadequately trained receptionist/front-desk personnel

Solution: Hire competent people for these frontline positions, provide them opportunities to learn and grow, and train them well to be prepared for all possible scenarios. They are your windows to the world.

Often, we make the dreadful mistake of hiring woefully inadequate people for receptionist positions and then fail to provide them with proper training and performance expectations. My own worst experience was being made to cool my heels at the front desk of a big-five accounting firm while the receptionist gossiped on the phone about a very steamy date she had the night before—and I had to listen to all the details!

Another common occurrence is for front-desk clerks in settings such as hotels to chitchat among themselves about other guests while you wait . . . and wait . . . to be checked in. I have actually heard comments such as "He is the guy with the cute butt" more than once. Although guests and visitors should be civil and patient and not beleaguer front-desk personnel, they should not be ignored or made to feel peripheral. These are the customers, after all. And the person standing in front of you should always have priority over someone on the phone.

To avoid such horror stories, I am in favor of hands-on actual practice sessions behind the front desk. Providing new personnel with a manual is just not adequate. If management treats the front desk as an important position, the receptionist will perform accordingly. Hire educated people and provide opportunities to move up quickly, or create a junior managerial position with other additional duties.

A professional receptionist should be well spoken, poised, conscious about appearance, cognizant of cultural differences and how to address people, and predisposed toward being helpful. Knowing a second language can be a real plus as well.

Problem: Frontline personnel who fail to listen attentively and respect visitors' needs and requests

Solution: A visitor's request should always be honored. For example, there's nothing more frustrating than arriving early so that you can pull yourself together, gather your thoughts, and get organized for an appointment—and then have the receptionist, who you told to give you some time, pick up the phone and announce your arrival as soon as you go to the rest room. Teach your receptionist to listen!

Problem: Keeping someone waiting for an appointment or rushing them along

Solution: Your visitor took the time to plan this session in advance, prepare for it, and show up on time to see you. Never, never keep someone with an appointment waiting—no matter how important you may think you are!

If there are time constraints, make them known up front when the appointment is scheduled. Say something like, "I can give you 30 minutes on Tuesday." If something has come up and you can't spend the promised time with your visitor, apologize and let her know politely—"Jean, I am sorry, but I have an emergency to deal with. Let's see what we can accomplish in 15 minutes."

Problem: Not properly escorting visitors in and out of your office

Solution: It makes a much nicer first impression to have the receptionist walk your visitor to your office, or to greet the visitor at the front desk yourself, than to have him wander through a strange maze armed only with hasty directions from the front desk.

If the visitor is escorted to your office by someone else, stand to greet him when he enters and walk around your desk to do it. (If you are a woman, you should stand to greet a male visitor as well!) The exception to this rule is when a coworker drops by; in this case, there is no need for such formality.

Don't position visitors across your desk, with you seated behind it. Have them sit at another table in your office. This is a gracious way of showing equality. If your office isn't equipped to allow this, book a conference room. Offer something to drink and serve it in a real glass or china cup.

Try to escort the visitor out, walking her to the elevator or front door, even if the office layout is simple. It is a gracious way to send her off and will leave a good last impression.

Problem: Receiving international guests in a cavalier, careless fashion

Solution: It is important that overseas visitors do not feel disrespected or that no one cares! If you are expecting dignitaries, trade delegations, or senior executives to visit and don't have a trained protocol person on staff, arrange for a high-level employee with international experience to meet them at the airport. Sometimes the CEO herself will go to greet the guest. Don't send an administrative assistant to do the job—comparable rank is called for here. Simply sending a limousine to pick up the guests is courting disaster; limo drivers are not what they used to be!

Sometimes you can work through a mayor's office to arrange an escort for the dignitaries from the plane and through immigrations and customs, after which you will take charge.

Know when visiting dignitaries will arrive at your headquarters and be sure that the chairman/CEO is in the lobby waiting to greet them if she has not gone to the airport. Even if the visitors are not top-level, you should have a qualified employee waiting for them in the lobby—it will make an enormous impression. Train everyone the visitors will come in contact with about proper forms of address, posture, dress, and cultural differences.

Problem: Inadequate attention to commonly accepted procedures for international business meetings

Solution: We U.S. Americans often are so casual in the workplace that we can easily be perceived by overseas visitors as ill-prepared and disrespectful. Do your homework to put your best foot forward and set a good impression from the start. Keep these tips in mind to ensure that the visit will go successfully:

- Set a mutually agreed-on timetable in advance and allow your visitors ample opportunity to rest from travel and time changes and to get adjusted. Not doing so will be perceived as attempting to take strategic advantage.

- Make sure that all printed material distributed is in the visitors' language as well as in your own. They probably speak English, but it is a gracious and respectful gesture; one prefers to read in one's mother language. Ask ahead if an interpreter will be needed. Some executives like to have one on hand anyway, so that if the visitors lapse into speaking their native language, one can find out later what was said.

- Have a seating plan observing hierarchy for the meeting with tent name cards and titles so there is no confusion when people arrive and no one's ego gets hurt. Usually, people from one company sit on one side and representatives from the other organization sit opposite them.

- Plan all meals with dietary restrictions in mind. You will incur hungry stomachs and piercing vibes if this is not observed. It truly is a mark of unsophistication when meals are not planned with different cultures in mind. Appropriate seating charts should be mapped out in advance, and nicely designed place cards and menu cards prepared. This ensures that people are strategically positioned to move business discussions along, and that the key players get to know one another as people.

- Always allow your guests to save face by preparing them ahead of their arrival for what will happen. Inform your guests in advance about any speeches, so that they are prepared to reply. Let them know if there will be a gift exchange, so that they are prepared to reciprocate. (Gifts are usually exchanged when a deal is signed or when negotiations have concluded.)

- Make sure that the visitors' hotel accommodations are acceptable. For example, someone should check prior to their arrival to see if they are smokers and are assigned the appropriate rooms.

- Find out whether spouses will accompany the guests and what type of program would be appropriate to plan for them. Don't just assign a low-level employee to take spouses shopping and museum-hopping. These days, spouses are savvy people who expect high-end activities to be arranged for them. A spouse who is a pediatric brain surgeon might want to meet his counterpart at a children's hospital; make the visit worthwhile.

Problem: Not paying attention to a strong overall departure (even if you feel that the deal may not be successful)

Solution: In the United States, we are savvy about closing deals when it comes to monetary concerns, but can be lacking in basic closing skills when it comes to more human concerns. Remember that a strong social closing will pay dividends and attend to farewell protocol with the utmost attention. Escort dignitaries to the airport to see them off—nothing closes a deal better than this gracious gesture. For visitors of lesser rank, a farewell in the lobby does wonders. Seeing them off in the taxi shows that you care for them as human beings and are not just after a deal! Overseas cultures are much more sensitive toward these gestures and their representatives will take note. Remember that to have a guest is a very important duty for a host at any level in the business world.

CHAPTER 5

Grooming and Appearance

This chapter is by Jill Bremer, AICI, CIP (© 2002 Jill Bremer). Jill Bremer is president of Bremer Communications and can be reached at <www.bremercommunications.com>. She is an image trainer, consultant, and Certified Image Professional (CIP) of the Association of Image Consultants International.

*Y*ou check your hair and makeup in the rearview mirror before leaving your car for what sounds like a promising interview. You look good and feel ready to make a good impression.

Much to your dismay, your first encounter inside the organization is with an indifferent receptionist sporting teased hair, long purple fingernails, and a tight T-shirt, who lets you cool your heels while she finishes a personal phone conversation. Eventually having captured her attention, you manage to garner cursory directions that propel you toward the Human Resources department. As you navigate the corporate maze by trial and error, you seek help from a young man in ripped blue jeans with greasy hair and a nose ring. Finally reaching your destination, you meet your interviewer, a middle-aged woman dressed in a tailored suit with a plunging neckline and arms weighted down with gold baubles that jangle with every expressive gesture. Perhaps this is not the ideal situation after all.

From bad breath to plunging necklines, slurping soup to presentation paralysis, I've seen it all. Since 1986, I have worked with individuals and organizations on their professional image, etiquette, and communication skills—often as the outside expert brought in by corporations to deal with indelicate issues, change old habits, and groom employees for success. My company offers workshops and coaching in the "soft" skills, often missing from the in-house training repertoire, that are so vital to creating and succeeding in a work environment characterized by civility.

While appearance codes often can be helpful in outlining proper dress and grooming for employees, they generally are vague and do not acknowledge cultural diversity. Employees feel left in the dark, and immigrants new to the United States feel confused or offended at the lack of sensitivity to their habits and values.

Having been born and raised in the United States and having worked primarily in the United States, it would be easy to fall into the trap of writing only for a U.S. audience or with a skew toward U.S. corporate values. We U.S. Americans all too frequently forget that people from other cultures have different values; what we find important may not be important to them. The result is mis-communication and misunderstanding.

Here we address some of the most common appearance and grooming challenges faced in today's workplace. Solutions are suggested to provide guidance to the manager or supervisor so that problems can be resolved and no longer will cause tension or incivility between workers. I also point out cultural, ethnic, or religious differences that should be taken into consideration before crafting corporate policy or passing judgment.

A specific appearance code is the best first step for any organization. While most people are familiar with dress codes, appearance codes go a step further by including guidelines for grooming (hair, makeup, nails, tattoos, fragrance, etc.). If an employee continues to push the limits regarding appropriate appearance and grooming, a private meeting with the individual may solve the problem. If the problem persists, an image coach is the answer. We can address the problem in a nonthreatening manner and provide solutions and guidance for the employee. In my work, I have found that a vast majority of people welcome the suggestions, and adjustments are made very quickly.

Casual Dress
A Recipe for Confusion

Problem: No clear guidelines for how to dress "business casual"

Solution: It used to be easy to get dressed for work. Take a suit, add a shirt and tie or blouse and jewelry, and you were ready to go. Not so today. The introduction of "business casual" has been a mixed blessing, adding more comfort and creativity, but also confusion and chaos. And don't think that business casual dress is limited to the United States; it is becoming acceptable in many other countries. An associate in India recently told me that young people in the computer industries there are now being encouraged to adopt the "Silicon Valley" attire of jeans, T-shirts, and sneakers. The challenge of dressing business casual is to not become too casual in other areas of work. Just as I believe "you are what you eat," so "you are what you wear." Recent studies have indicated that employee morale and productivity are no better because of a dress-down policy. In fact, many of my clients have told me they are revising their dress codes to reflect traditional business dress.

The problem with business casual is that we were never taught how to dress that way. A wealth of information is available on traditional business dress, but very little on how to dress both casually and professionally. In my seminars, I teach three different levels of business casual dress—each may be appropriate depending on the situation, objective, and industry.

The rule of thumb is: The more you deal with a client's money, future, or family, the more conservative a role you should present. Industries such as finance, law, accounting, health care, and insurance should project a conservative, traditional image to the public. Here business casual may be limited to Fridays only. More relaxed industries, such as computer, high-tech, real estate, travel, manufacturing, publishing, and education, can present a more casual image and usually accept some level of business casual on a daily basis. Those in creative industries, such as advertising, public relations, and entertainment, should choose clothes that reflect the latest trends. This may be a blend of traditional with business casual, but it should always have a fashion-forward look.

The first step to getting properly dressed is to determine your activities and responsibilities for that particular day, always keeping in mind your industry, your company's written (or unwritten) dress code, and your position within the organization. You can then choose one of three levels of business casual dress. Of course, traditional business ensembles of suits for men and skirted suits for women may also be the choice for given days or activities. The bottom line is that dressing for work has become situational and you need a bit of everything in your closet these days.

!@!%#!@!%#!@!%#!@!%#!@!%#!@!%#!@!%#!@!%#!@!%#!@!%#!@!%#!@!

Questions to Ask Yourself before You Choose the Day's Mode of Dress

1. What are my activities for the day?

2. With whom will I be interacting?

3. Where will I be meeting them?

4. What will my clients be wearing?

5. What will my superiors be wearing?

6. What will my coworkers be wearing?

The Three Levels of Business Casual

Basic Business Casual: Most Informal, for "Backstage" Days

Basic business casual, the most casual style of business casual dress, is the level of choice for those days in the office when you'll be working without client contact. It may also be appropriate for some informal off-site training sessions, retreats, or company-sponsored sporting events. This relaxed level of dressing may be appropriate on a daily basis for less-traditional industries; it depends on the guidelines of the particular organization. This mode consists of ensembles made up of only two pieces—a top and a bottom. No jacket is necessary, nor is wearing a collar of any kind. Men or women can choose casual pants (jeans would depend on your corporate culture) and add a short- or long-sleeve shirt, high-quality T-shirt, knit top, or sweater. Women also can choose a casual skirt and top, a casual dress, or a jumper.

Standard Business Casual: Middle Ground for Casual Meetings and Workshops

When people hear the term *business casual,* they most often visualize the middle level of standard business casual, which consists of a top and bottom teamed with a third piece. This mode of dress, worn on a daily basis for less-formal industries and on Casual Fridays in some traditional industries, is appropriate for meetings within the company when you know others will be similarly dressed or for off-site workshops and conferences. Standard business casual features styling more tailored than basic business casual in fabrics such as wools, wool blends, silk blends, microfiber, and twills. The additional layer, which can be in the form of a casual, unstructured jacket, cardigan or pullover sweater, tie, scarf, or vest, adds a professional touch to tailored pants or skirts teamed with a casual shirt, knit top, or fine-gauge sweater. For men, a collar is always included in these ensembles, if not in the shirt beneath, then in a jacket on top.

Executive Business Casual: Tailored, but a Bit Less Formal Than Traditional

Executive business casual, the most formal mode of business casual dress, is very close to traditional business dress. It features luxurious fabrics, such as wools, cashmere, silks, and linens, expert tailoring, and a contemporary flair that conveys influence. It can be worn when meeting with business casual clients, making a presentation, or leading a meeting. Those in conservative fields will choose this level for Casual Fridays if they have any client contact or are in a leadership position. Creative industries often wear executive business casual on a daily basis. This level requires a structured jacket at all times, but not necessarily a tie. Men may choose sports coats or blazers, pants in wool, silk, linen, or blends, solid or patterned shirts or fine-gauge knit, cashmere, or silk sweaters. Women should select matched or unmatched pantsuits in wool, linen, silk, or blends. Skirts may be teamed with separate jackets. Appropriate tops include fine-gauge knits, cotton, linen, silk, and cashmere.

A word of warning: Never make the mistake of dressing too casually for any business situation. Dressing down too far can cost you customers, jobs, promotions, and opportunities. Better to exceed expectations and "dress for where you're going, not for where you're at." Traditional business dress will always be the best choice for communicating leadership and authority.

The following are other common problems related to appearance that crop up in today's workplace.

Problem: Wearing wrinkled, stained, or foul-smelling clothes

Solution: Whether you're wearing traditional business dress or business casual, wrinkled, dirty, or smelly clothing is a sure image killer.

!@!%#!@!%#!@!%#!@!%#!@!%#!@!%#!@!%#!@!%#!@!%#!@!%#!@!%#!@!

Inappropriate Clothing for the Workplace

One medical firm told me about an employee who rode his bike to work and then proceeded to wear his padded biking shorts and skintight shirt for the rest of day. A private conversation with that individual solved the problem. To save your employees from this type of embarrassment, here is my list of business casual don'ts:

Sweatshirts
T-shirts bearing slogans
Sleeveless tops for men
Midriff-baring tops and halter tops
Spaghetti-strap tops
Blue jeans*
Sweatpants
Leggings/stirrup pants
Shorts
Miniskirts
Athletic shoes
Thong or athletic sandals*
Work boots
Bare legs*
Zip-front hooded sweatshirt jackets
Team jackets, jean jackets
Overalls
Biking shorts
See-through tops

The best advice for Casual Fridays is to dress only one or two levels below how you normally dress.

*Wearing jeans or sandals or showing bare legs can be controversial; consider your corporate culture and position carefully before choosing these. They may be acceptable for informal industries or for Casual Fridays.

Many of us don't clean or launder our clothes nearly often enough. The best way to care for many items of apparel is to routinely have them cleaned and pressed by a dry cleaner you've come to trust. Regular cleaning can remove stains and eliminate odors created by perspiration, body oils, and skin cells. It also rids your clothes of such atmospheric soils as dust, which can act as an abrasive and damage fibers. Don't have your clothes pressed but not cleaned. There may be stains on the clothing that are invisible to the eye, such as ginger ale and tonic water, which the hot pressing machines will set on the fabric, making them almost impossible to remove later.

Between cleanings, wool garments should be hung out overnight before being put back in the closet. Wool is a resilient fabric and will return to its natural shape if allowed to breathe.

A laundry service is the best choice for men's business shirts and cotton pants. A combination of light or medium starch and pressing creates a crisp, professional appearance.

The advent of spray-on wrinkle reducers may be the answer for clothes that need a quick touch-up. My clients report excellent results with these products and recommend them highly to those who travel.

Suggestive Clothing
That's Not the Impression You Want to Make

Problem: Wearing suggestive clothing in the workplace

Solution: This is more of a problem for females than males in the United States. Men have set the standards of business dress in this country for more than a century, making any choice a woman makes "marked." Too conservative, too trendy, too drab, too colorful, too loose, too tight—whichever she chooses can be seen as a negative by someone else.

In the 1970s and 1980s, U.S. American women were encouraged to wear ensembles that mimicked their male counterparts. Today, these same women feel freer to dress in a style that reflects their femininity, but in doing so they also run the risk of having their choices misunderstood. What is not considered suggestive by the wearer may well be by someone else in the office.

My answer to this dilemma has to do with skin. The sight of bare skin can be evocative to others. It suggests intimacy and is more appropriately revealed in our personal lives than in our business lives. For the workplace, choose long sleeves over sleeveless, knee-length skirts over minis, closed shoes over sandals, hose over bare legs, one button undone rather than two or three. Sheer or other see-through clothing should be avoided, unless one wishes to be talked about over the watercooler for months to come. Bare midriffs may be gaining popularity, but should never be shown at work, no matter what your generation.

A woman's professional image can easily be damaged at after-hours events. One of my law firm clients told me they once had a female partner whose everyday dress was classic conservative but who arrived for a gala in a tight, low-cut evening gown. Her credibility and integrity suddenly came into question. The same can happen to the bikini-wearing executive at the company picnic. Never forget that these events are official functions of the organization—dress accordingly. Tasteful choices that leave something to the imagination are best.

With that said, consider professional attire in countries other than the United States. Carol Jungman of Cendant Intercultural, The Bennett Group, who is a cross-cultural training consultant, says: "In many European countries, individuality is expressed through dress and females enjoy a broader range of fashion for the workplace. What they see as individual flair or a feminine touch, U.S. companies view as too sexy."

Jungman also points out that in some parts of Europe, clothes are not considered as significant or as important to one's acceptance or success. For instance, it's not unusual for workers to wear the same outfit two or three days in a row with no ill effect. And in countries where citizens don't have a comparable level of disposable income or conveniences, dress habits might reflect that reality (e.g., mismatched outfits, out-of-style clothing, socks instead of hose). She suggests U.S. companies overseas define as specifically as possible the acceptable guidelines for dress in their places of business. Whatever is left unsaid will surely be worn to work.

Slogans
Save It for Later!

Problem: Wearing an item of clothing that bears a slogan or message inappropriate for the workplace

Solution: Shirts with slogans are only appropriate at work when that slogan communicates the marketing message or logo of the company—and then only when that organization has deemed it permissible. Any other slogan runs the risk of offending someone else. Those who feel a need to express their personal views on their clothing should do so during nonbusiness hours. They may argue that the sayings are expressions of free speech, but just as with tattoos, U.S. courts rarely uphold those arguments. Appearance codes must offer specific guidelines for wearing slogans in the workplace.

Clothing for Videoconferencing
Keep It Solid and Simple

Problem: Wearing unsuitable clothing for on-camera situations

Solution: Dressing for a videoconference presents special challenges. The camera is sensitive to color, pattern, and reflection. Care must be taken to select clothing and accessories that play well to the camera and to the audience. To look wrinkle-free, choose wool, silk, knit, or cashmere garments. Solid-color suits with moderate shaping and padding are the best choices. Any shade of blue works well on camera; other good colors include dark reds, teal, dark greens, deep purples, and rich browns. Avoid bright red, bright yellow, lime green, pure white, and black.

Shirts and blouses should be off-white or pastel. Plaids, stripes, dots, and checks are not camera-friendly; they take on a life of their own. Buttons and jewelry should be brushed metal or nonreflective. Women should avoid wearing large jewelry and dangling earrings. Select ties and scarves with small prints. The rule for dressing for any camera is to keep it solid and simple.

Excessive Jewelry
Overkill

Problem: Wearing too much jewelry to work

Solution: Consider jewelry the final, subtle touch that completes a professional wardrobe. Multiple rings, bracelets, and necklaces can get in the way of your work and project an image of being ostentatious or extreme. Too many rings become painful in a handshake. Too many bracelets hinder computer and telephone work. Too many necklaces can be noisy and catch on a desk.

I advise my clients to wear only one ring per hand. A single bracelet or a few thin ones are best. One necklace or a few strands together look professional. Post earrings are preferred over drop styles.

Tie tacks and tie bars are currently out of fashion for men; keep neckties secure by tucking the narrow end through the label on the underside of the wide end. Cuff links are always in style for French cuffs. Choose small, conservative styles in metal or silk rope.

Watches for both men and women should be the highest quality one can afford. Thin styles are preferred over heavier styles, sport watches, or novelty watches.

I advise recent college graduates to not wear any college jewelry so interviewers and employers are not reminded how new to the workforce the graduates are.

Head Coverings
Be Sensitive to Cultural Differences

Problem: Vague guidelines for head coverings in the workplace

Solution: Many religions, such as Islam, Judaism, and Sikhism, as well as the Amish and Mennonites, incorporate head coverings as signs of deference and devotion. Head coverings indicate that those who wear them are ambassadors of their beliefs and accountable for their actions. Orthodox and conservative groups often require that head coverings are worn at all times; most reformed religions require that head coverings are worn only for worship services or religious holidays.

Dress codes I have seen issued by U.S. businesses rarely mention head coverings. If the topic is referred to at all, it lists only hats and caps as unacceptable for the workplace. Employers should review their appearance codes and amend them if necessary. Policies need to address the issue of head coverings in detail, taking into consideration that some are worn for religious reasons and cannot be excluded from the workplace. Coworkers and employers should never stare at or joke about someone's head covering. Sensitivity and tolerance toward another's beliefs must be shown.

Tattoos and Piercings
The Politics of Body Art

Problem: Exposed tattoos and piercings

Solution: Tattoos and body piercings may be signs of self-expression, but they can hurt one's chances for employment and career advancement.

Recent surveys show that those in positions to hire are less likely to employ someone with visible tattoos or piercings. Survey findings also reveal that many managers hold lower opinions of someone based on his or her body art or nonear piercings. In my work with organizations in conservative industries, managers say they question the judgment of someone who knowingly rocks the boat by exposing their piercings or tattoos at work. They feel these mixed messages are disconcerting to customers and not commensurate with the overall organizational image.

Unless one is part of a creative industry, such as entertainment, music, or the arts, tattoos and body piercings trigger negative first impressions and erode confidence in the abilities of the individual. Perceived as a sign of rebellion, many also associate tattoos with criminals; in fact, most gang members imprint themselves with signs of affiliation, violent images, or inflammatory words.

In conservative industries, women with multiple ear piercings should limit earrings to one per ear and men should remove all earrings. If one has tattoos or nonear piercings, my recommendation is to keep them out of sight while at work. There are too many risks involved with having them visible—denied business opportunities, hassles from supervisors, exclusion from special events, even being fired, or not getting hired in the first place. Rulings by U.S. courts have traditionally been in favor of the employer, even when the employee says he's being singled out or claims body art or piercings as an expression of free speech.

I advise employers in conservative industries to include in their appearance codes recommendations that tattoos and body piercings be hidden at work, or at least when interacting with customers. The code should include the business reasons for the position: safety, hygiene, and corporate image. Keep in mind that if there are religious or ethnic reasons for the body art, discrimination on these grounds is illegal. Freedom of expression is encouraged, however, in creative industries. Toleration, even celebration, of tattoos and body art is usually part of these corporate cultures.

Working Out
Hit the Showers

Problem: Unpleasant body odors

Solution: Because of the popularity of undertaking physical exercise during work hours, body odor can become a very real problem among coworkers. Bathing is a necessity after any work-out, even a lunchtime jog, and employees may need to be reminded to hit the showers. One might not think it would be necessary to belabor the point, but complaints about inadequate personal hygiene and its resulting body odor are on the rise in the workplace.

Differing perceptions and tolerance of body smells may also be marks of cultural or religious distinctions. For instance, some conservative and orthodox religions observe holidays that dictate no bathing. On the other hand, Islam places a great emphasis on cleanliness. Muslims are required to bathe some or all of their body before each of the five daily prayers. Supervisors, coworkers, and policies alike must be sensitive to these differences. Many Europeans believe U.S. Americans have absurd attitudes about cleanliness and that we are hyperclean. In some cultures, a little body odor is considered natural and does not offend.

When immigrants come to the United States, their sense of cleanliness might not match that of U.S. Americans. U.S. employers should be sensitive to this cultural difference and create specific appearance codes with explicit guidelines for cleanliness, or simply encourage a tolerant climate in which people are comfortable with others' grooming habits.

And for the employee who likes to remove his or her shoes during the workday, foot odor can be quite offensive to fellow workers. Dealing with personal odors can be a touchy subject. Managers should talk privately with the individual and approach these situations with sensitivity, empathy, and directness. Like the person who wears too much cologne, people often are not aware of the extent of the problem. While they may at first be shocked or offended, more often than not they appreciate the heads-up and will quickly make the necessary adjustments.

Mouth
Bad Breath, Bad Vibes

Problem: Offensive breath

Solution: There's little worse than having a conversation with someone who has foul-smelling breath. Bad breath, or halitosis, happens to everyone at some point. The familiar mouthwashes only mask bad breath for a short time and, because of the alcohol they contain, actually dry out mouth tissues even more, which brings the odor back with a vengeance. Sprays, mints, and gum contain sugar, which can also exacerbate the problem.

A breath problem in the workplace is an issue best discussed in private, but I suggest to clients that they keep a toothbrush and toothpaste in their desk at work to brush after eating, a suggestion that can also be included in a company's appearance code.

Grooming
Less Is More

Problem: Wearing too much makeup

Solution: A woman with overdone makeup is unattractive at any age. Makeup application is an art and, unfortunately, most women fall victim to products and styles not suitable for their coloring, age, or skill level. Practice makes perfect, along with some professional input whenever possible. A professional color analysis consultation is the first step to determining the most flattering makeup colors to wear. Some women prefer not to wear makeup; however, they should look to their corporate culture before doing without makeup at work.

Problem: Fingernails that are too long or unkempt

Solution: Hands and fingernails are noticed by others and contribute to one's professional image. No matter what industry or position the employee is in, fingernails must be cared for on a regular basis, either by the individual or by a nail-care professional. In general, men's nails should be short and clean, and filed smooth with no ragged cuticles. Women's cuticles should be smooth and nails should match in length; if women choose to wear polish, it must be maintained or removed as soon as it chips.

In conservative industries, women should have nails that extend no longer than about ¼ inch beyond the fingertip. Colors can be light or dark in the traditional shades of pink, red, rose, peach, and coral. Avoid trendy colors at work, as well as artistic designs and appliqués. A pedicure is a must for any professional woman who wears sandals or open-toe shoes to the office. In more informal or liberal industries, longer nail lengths are usually acceptable, along with trendy colors, designs, and appliqués.

Problem: Wearing too much fragrance

Solution: Working and interacting in close quarters can cause tension among workers, which can be easily aggravated by smells. Perfumes, colognes, hair products, as well as food and body odors bring an assortment of aromas into the office.

U.S. Americans are sensitive to fragrance in the workplace. To people of French, Italian, and Arab descent, though, fragrance is very important; many don't feel completely dressed without adding perfume. Employers need to be aware of these cultural differences.

My advice has always been to not wear fragrance in business settings, certainly never for first-impression situations. Too many risks are associated with scent. Because fragrance is more noticeable to others than it is to the wearer, it can easily overpower or offend another person. In fact, I know of one person who lost a job opportunity because her choice of perfume reminded the interviewer of his ex-wife!

As with so many elements of grooming and appearance in the office, less is more. If you must wear fragrance, do so lightly. Consider wearing a scented skin lotion instead of perfume or cologne.

If you are allergic to fragrance, you must make coworkers, clients, and vendors aware of this fact.

C H A P T E R   6

Conflict Management

You join the department as a newly hired manager and inherit a reasonably professional staff. However, a couple of employees seem to be constantly at loggerheads with one another. The office is sometimes quite tense because of these two. It is now your responsibility to identify coaching and other tools to resolve their feuding so that the rest of the department can function. You are realistic enough to know, however, that putting out this fire will not ensure a conflict-free environment. Other differences likely will arise. Better to have some resolution techniques in place for the department as a whole.

Conflicts: You Can't Do Away with Them

No matter how hard we try to create an atmosphere that nurtures consensus building and collaboration, misunderstandings are bound to arise and tempers do flair on occasion. Even the nicest, kindest people find themselves embroiled in a conflict from time to time. Most organizations do not want to admit this and don't provide employees with the tools to properly prepare for these eventualities. The key is to recognize that a problem exists, to know how to find a resolution before the situation escalates and deteriorates, and to normalize the relationship and move on.

First: Take a Personal Inventory and
Make a Realistic Appraisal

An important first step in learning how to resolve conflict is to sort out in your own mind what you bring to the situation. Ask yourself these questions:

- What constitutes conflict for me?

- How do I like to resolve differences? Depersonalize conflicts?

- Do I have a capacity for empathy?

- Do I believe that everyone has a right to express themselves without fear of retaliation?

- Do I think that airing feelings openly and honestly is beneficial?

- Do I consider it acceptable to snap, threaten, and yell at colleagues and subordinates in the workplace?

- Do I often inflict pain on others?

- Am I indifferent to the feelings of others?

Once you have answered the questions honestly and identified areas where there is a need for improvement, start looking for solutions. Can your training department provide them? Do you need a coach? What tools would help you work these things through?

Let's examine the communications skills that are most needed to manage conflict.

Assertive Anger: Learn How to Express Anger Nonthreateningly

Anger is a natural emotion designed to aid your survival when you need to carry on and heal. It is different from *aggression,* which is a behavior or action taken as a consequence of feeling angry. Some communications experts say that you are the owner of anger and you must decide whether to be angry or not. This is difficult, because anger is a feeling. But where you can be in control at the workplace is regarding how you express anger—namely, learning to express it in a nonthreatening and nonaggressive manner. Try to communicate very clearly what is making you angry. Timing is important. Do not hesitate; always speak up as soon as an incident that makes you angry has occurred.

Some materials on conflict management teach that the best way to do so is to use "I" language, but I have always found this labeling a bit confusing. I prefer using "me" language for conveying how a coworker's problematic actions make you feel and how you would like to resolve the problem (rather than just using "you" language to accuse the individual). Here are two examples:

1. "Yelling over the cubicle walls disrupts my concentration and frustrates me. Please stop doing that. Walking over will be less disruptive."

2. "Coming into work late every day makes me fall behind in my work. Please follow the rules and try to come in on time."

Your tone and the volume of your voice should not be intimidating when you convey these messages. A frown is fine, for it will help support the meaning of your words. Try not to be sarcastic and never use put-downs or make accusations such as, "When you come in late, you p--s me off. Who do you think you are, royalty?" This will only escalate the conflict, because you are not separating the problem from the personality. Figure 6.1 illustrates the steps through which conflicts escalate and identifies

FIGURE 6.1   The Escalating Ladder of Incivility

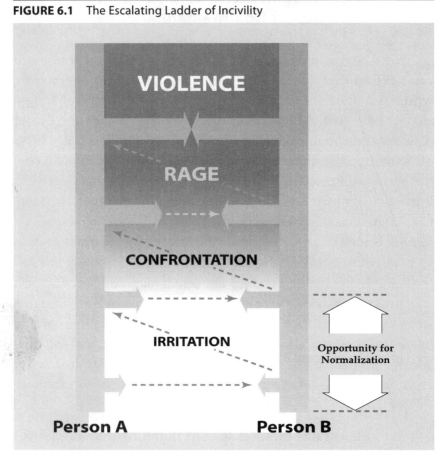

Source: © 2001 Giovinella Gonthier, Civility Associates. E-mail: civilityassoc@hotmail.com

where in the process it is readily possible to diffuse conflict and normalize relations.

Active Listening: What's She Really Saying?

The best way to diffuse a conflict situation when someone is angry with you—whether she has asked you in "me" language to stop doing something that is annoying her ("Yelling over the cubicle walls frustrates me.") or is making heated accusations ("You idiot, stop yelling over the cubicle walls like a f----g maniac!")—is to use active listening, which entails three components:

1. Acknowledge the feeling. What is she feeling? Why is she calling me an idiot? Have I been acting like one?

2. Acknowledge the content. What is the real issue here? Do I have to restate what I think I heard? (Do this only if you honestly need clarification, not to be cheeky.)

3. Acknowledge the solution. What can be done to find a solution or to prevent this from happening again? Apologizing is a quick way to let the person know that you accept there is a problem.

As you proceed through these acknowledgment steps, *always keep your cool and lower your voice!* Saying something like, "Golly, I am sorry if it makes you frustrated. I did not realize that my yelling over the cubicle walls disturbed you. I will try to stop doing it," will help diffuse the situation fast, especially if you take the necessary action *because you are empathizing.*

If you focus on the person rather than on the situation, responding angrily to an accusatory remark, "Yeah, b---h. You think your foul mouth doesn't make you sound like a f----g maniac? Stop telling me what to do," it will only escalate the conflict and make it harder to normalize the relationship later on. If her dirty language upsets you, bring it to her attention immediately after the next time she uses it rather than now, when she has raised an issue with you.

Receptivity to Mending: Let's Get Back to Normal

After an incident has occurred, you should be open to mending the situation. This is called *normalizing.* If you find it difficult to apologize verbally, send a note. Or send flowers. But do something to get across the idea that you wish to mend the relationship.

Some people, especially men, do not like to have a "bad be-havior" discussion. Instead of apologizing, they will invite you to play golf or go to a ball game. Don't dig in your heels and say, "I want an apology, damn it!" Remember, we are all different and re-spond to situations in diverse ways. See the invitation as someone else's way of reaching out to mend the relationship. Open your-self to any type of apology that comes your way. If your leader in-vites you to lunch but never says, "I am sorry," let it go.

!@!%#!@!%#!@!%#!@!%#!@!%#!@!%#!@!%#!@!%#!@!%#!@!%#!@!%#!@!

Try the Following When You Have a Disagreement with Someone

1. State your message in "me" language that expresses your feelings, not in accusatory "you" language.

2. Detach from yourself and listen to the other party without interrupting.

3. Restate what you think you have heard.

4. If you do not understand, ask questions to clarify.

5. Try not to be obstinate.

6. Do not attack the person—avoid barbs and mind your tone of voice.

7. Keep focused on the current problem (stay in today) and do not bring up the past (yesterday).

8. Be reasonable.

9. Accept that you can do something wrong or have a habit that others find irritating.

10. Apologize—that diffuses tension fast.

It is important to stay in today and to see incidents that have already occurred as past. If someone who has torn you apart at a meeting comes into your office later and says, "I dug in too deeply at the meeting. I see now that you had a point. I am sorry," respond, "Thanks for the apology. Next time, can we avoid personal attacks in public?" A situation like this reminds us not to be so pigheaded at meetings. Think before you dig your heels in too deeply.

My advice is to always try to accept an apology. If the same bad behavior happens over and over again, then you have to put a stop to it. Go and see the person in his office and tell him that the pattern of frequent outbursts and subsequent apologies has to stop and that you would like him to make a sincere effort to change his negative behavior. If you apologize to someone and they start screaming at you, just say, "Let's talk about it again later." Then walk away.

Three Sides to a Conflict: Seek Help for a Stalemate

Sometimes, no matter how hard you try, you still aren't able to resolve the situation. It is always said that there are two sides to a conflict. I teach that, in fact, there are three. Figure 6.2 illustrates the third side, the community, in which any conflict takes place. When all personal attempts at resolving a dispute have failed, ask someone at work to see that your conflict is mediated or arbitrated.

Mediation: Help in Reaching an Agreement

A *mediator* helps both sides seek an agreement that is *mutually* satisfactory. The mediator lets both sides speak or shuttles between offices during an agreed-on time frame, so that there can be no delaying tactics. She probes for reasons behind each person's position and discusses how to arrive at a solution. Both sides have to agree to the solution—and not blame the mediator later on.

FIGURE 6.2   Three Sides to a Conflict

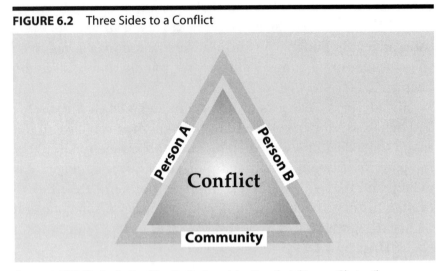

Source: © 2001 Giovinella Gonthier, Civility Associates. E-mail: civilityassoc@hotmail.com

Arbitration: Letting Someone Else Decide

An *arbiter* is a neutral third person whose judgment is final. This condition must be accepted by both sides prior to the decision. The arbiter listens to both sides and makes a decision based on fairness; once again, a time frame is important. Remember, the decision is final—do not hate the arbiter after the judgment has been handed down.

Alternative Dispute Resolution: Yet Another Option

Some organizations offer yet another option for settling conflicts between managers and workers over policy disputes. Alternative dispute resolutions are less expensive than going through the court system and the resolutions are kept internal instead of becoming public documents. Many allow you to be represented by an attorney.

Violence: Businesses Need to Take Precautions

Although incivility of varying degrees is a more common occurrence, violence does take place in the workplace. According to Kroll Associates, a New York–based security firm, more than two million violent crimes occur each year in the workplace. These include murders, rapes, and other assaults. This is also a topic that must be considered, because unchecked incivility can lead to violent situations.

Just as wise organizations do not wait for incivility to rear its ugly head before putting a civility program in place, effective leaders do not wait for a violent incident to occur before putting a threat-management procedure into place. They act to preempt such incidents.

The best violence-prevention program that I have seen is Boeing's Managing Workplace Violence program. To create a safe environment for employees and visitors to Boeing's many sites, the company has distributed reader-friendly brochures to all its staff, trained each employee to be aware of and to respond to workplace violence, and created multidisciplinary Threat Management Teams ready to provide immediate response to a violent threat, investigate the incident, and assist victims.

Boeing's definition of the workplace includes regular offices, field locations, temporary offices, parking lots, and travel between workplace locations. Threats are defined as including any assault, stalking, unwelcome touching, bullying, intimidating demeanor or comments (written or verbal), implied threat by course of conduct or domestic abuse, as well as any behavior that creates concern for personal safety, including throwing objects, destroying property, or possessing weapons.

Including domestic abuse is crucial and still cutting edge. Most people are not aware that the leading cause of occupational death for women is homicide! Kroll Associates estimates that husbands and boyfriends commit 13,000 acts of violence against women in the workplace each year. Having as simple a plan in place as how to exit the building when employees are in danger can prevent catastrophe.

!@!%#!@!%#!@!%#!@!%#!@!%#!@!%#!@!%#!@!%#!@!%#!@!%#!@!%#!@!

Boeing Company Employees Have Been Taught to Heed These Warning Signs of Violence

1. Threats to cause harm

2. Bizarre or unusual conduct

3. Angry, volatile outbursts

4. Perceived persecution or victimization

5. Excessive talk about weapons

6. Uncharacteristic attendance problems

7. Lack of concern for personal safety

Although Boeing acknowledges that not everyone who exhibits warning signs of violence is a risk to the workplace, it emphasizes that an employee's awareness and evaluation can make a crucial difference. Employees are advised to act immediately and to know exactly where and to whom to report. Their training includes competencies on how to stay calm and how to handle a person threatening violence—such as don't touch the person, don't argue, and don't be condescending.

In today's high-pressure world, one needs to understand that even good people can snap. Knowing what to do and how to do it is the best deterrent to a violent situation and will greatly affect the outcome. If your organization does not have procedures established to identify, assess, and respond to threats or incidents of violence in the workplace, ask for them to be put into place. Emergency drills for all types of scenarios are a matter of necessity. Perhaps the events of September 11, 2001, will make us all think twice about being prepared.

CHAPTER 7

Systemic Change: Implementing a Civility Policy in the Workplace

*Y*ou *are invited to make a presentation to some corporate officials on teaching a civility course at their site. Halfway through, a manager who noisily arrived late blurts out, "No one is interested in this!" and leaves the room. You feel like saying, "And I rest my case." Instead, you look at the group, regain your composure, and proceed as your good judgment tells you that you should. You apologize for the interruption and continue with the presentation matter-of-factly. Another senior officer stops you and says, "No, I must apologize on behalf of our company for what has happened. Believe me, the rest of us are interested and want to hear more. This incident confirms our need for this type of training. Would you like to take a break before continuing?" Civility has triumphed and your faith is restored! (Based on the author's personal experience.)*

The goal of any business is to produce and sell the products and services in which it specializes. There is a bottom-line cost to incivility that adversely affects this goal. It only stands to reason that implementing a civility campaign will have a long-lasting positive influence on business performance. I must emphasize once again that it is cost-effective to be proactive and put a civility program into place before an incident has occurred or a lawsuit has been filed. Once you put procedures in place for promoting civil behavior in your company, the number and severity of complaints about incivility will decline—after a successful civility initiative has been in place for about a year.

Organizational Implementation: It Takes the Whole Village

For a company to truly embrace civility requires the support and participation of every single division and all the employees, senior executives to administrative assistants, vice presidents to line personnel, managers to maintenance staff. Once the entire community is involved, individuals will reinforce and support one another's efforts.

If we accept as a given that civility is good business, the challenge becomes how to design a campaign to constantly reinforce the principles of civility within the organization. In *Lessons from the Top: The 50 Most Successful Business Leaders in America— and What You Can Learn from Them*, by Thomas J. Neff and James M. Citrin (Doubleday, 2001), former General Electric CEO John "Jack" Welch, Jr. advised: "Pick a theme every few years, and rally the entire company around it." Sound advice—and the time is right to make civility the theme.

The question then is just how does one rally a community around an idea? There has to be a coordinated effort, starting with the CEO and division leaders, who should now include civility on all their staff meeting agendas to ignite a spark. Employees will slowly get used to the idea that change of significant magnitude is coming their way (instead of changing the tire of a car, they are going to build an entirely new car).

Although a CEO is the sponsor of the new theme, a designated person has to actually administer the program and coordinate with all division heads and employees in general. This person can be from the Quality, Human Resources, or Protocol department, or a consultant brought on board for a specific duration of time. Implementation does not take place by osmosis!

The objective is to begin to change the way workers talk about the issue of civility. Gradually, they will stop making fun of the concept and start to think about just how this change will affect their interactions with one another and with clients. They will question how their performance abilities and personal accountability may change. Get the whole staff buzzing. Create a special e-mail conversation on the subject among employees. Ask them to consider how incorporating civility will improve quality and excellence at work, grow more profit, acquire and retain new customers, contribute to their wellness and friendships at work, and enhance their personal professional skills.

Implementation must be reinforced on several different fronts. Many organizations now refer to a system of "levers" that they use to implement any systemic change, including a civility/respect program. The idea is to work continually at aligning these levers and keeping them in balance. The levers include:

- Leadership—Top executives need both to talk about civility and to behave in a way that sets a positive example.

- Education and Training—Civility training (not just patterned niceness) must be instituted, and respect should be a component of all other training programs.

- Measurement—Progress should be monitored on an ongoing basis through 360-degree feedback and company-wide surveys.

- Methods and Processes—Special sets of tools that support civility need to be designed, such as Sprint's handbook tips for successfully running civil meetings or Southwest Airlines' note cards for employees to recognize one another's acts of kindness.

- Resources—The civility campaign must be budgeted for, and needed books, other resource materials, and consultation provided.

- Rewards and Recognition—Positive reinforcement methods should be in place through which management can reward civility and integrate civility components in performance appraisals.

Leaders: They Need to "Walk the Talk"

The most crucial factor in successfully implementing a civility program is to have the organization's leaders demonstrate civil and professional behavior. They must walk the talk, enforce the policies, and set the examples. When senior management communicates civility messages face-to-face with units or departments, employees believe that the message is important.

I hold up Sprint as an example through much of this section because the global communications giant is at the forefront of civility philosophy and implementation and has put together an exemplary program. Although many organizations pay lip service to the concept of "Respect for People," which is the name of Sprint's civility program, few have effective organizationwide programs in place and concrete examples to emulate. Marty Lustig, the Assistant Vice President of Quality for Sprint, summed up the importance of leadership nicely when he advised me that you have to "watch the feet and the lips" of senior management. In another interview, Jodie Solow, Director of Organizational Development at the Blue Cross Blue Shield Association, echoed the same sentiments.

Lack of civility in interpersonal relationships is bad behavior, pure and simple, whether it's the receptionist or the CEO who is behaving badly. Carrying on angrily diminishes both of the participants in such an exchange. It is counterproductive and poisons the air. A true leader, by demonstrating civility, creates an environment in which both interpersonal relationships and organizational performance are enhanced. A leader does not talk down to a subordinate in public, but discusses the issues with the individual behind closed doors. A leader does not blow up at customers or hide behind defective goods, but becomes part of the solution. The philosopher Goethe said, "The way you see someone is the way you treat them. And how you treat them is what they become."

Policies: Put It in Writing

A good employee handbook with an explicit civility policy detailing how employees are expected to treat one another is a key part of the educational process. The simple step of giving civility (or respect, as some choose to call it) its own listing in the index of a company handbook will underscore how important the issue is to the organization. The way the policy is written can also be helpful to its implementation. Avoid legalistic language and jargon. Clear and concise writing will help prevent misunderstandings.

Please tailor a policy to your company's needs. One size does *not* fit all. You should be able to show that you can identify the problem and follow through with consequences. If you consistently demonstrate that you will protect the targets of incivility and that there is a very real possibility of punishment for the instigators because of zero tolerance, the bad behavior will start to go away.

Although it is critical for civility to be mentioned in an organization's policy manual because it sets an initial level of expectation and provides legal protection in the eventuality of a lawsuit, it is insufficient as a lone tool for promoting civility. There is a limit to the effectiveness of policies. By themselves, they are not going to prevent the problem from recurring and may even provide the illusion that the problem has been tackled. You have to start ingraining it in employees' minds by providing them with competency tools. You also need to enforce your policies.

!@!%#!@!%#!@!%#!@!%#!@!%#!@!%#!@!%#!@!%#!@!%#!@!%#!@!%#!@!%#!@!

Sample Civility Policy

This is a policy that I have recommended to some companies:

Civility is valued here. We are dedicated to maintaining a workplace that is both productive and civil. Our employees will treat colleagues, other coworkers and personnel, our internal/external customers, and the public with respect. We encourage courteous and positive communication and will not tolerate belittling, rude, hostile, and volatile behavior. Vulgar language and gestures are not conducive to a reasonable and satisfactory work environment. Settle disagreements by discussion and intervention. If you feel that you are disrespected in any way, please document the situation with the pertinent facts and report it immediately to your direct supervisor or to your contact representative/harassment support officer and/or the Human Resources department.

Individuals engaging in any type of incivility will face immediate disciplinary action, which may include termination.

(A reporting mechanism must be stated clearly in your handbook. A recent study by psychologist Lilia Cortina of the University of Michigan at Ann Arbor and her team, which I discussed in Chapter 2, demonstrated a direct link between the failure to do anything about maltreatment in the workplace and such mental health complications as anxiety and depression ["Incivility in the Workplace: Incidence and Impact," *Journal of Occupational Health Psychology* 6, no. 1, 2001].)

Training: Provide the Resources Needed to Effect Change

Although interpersonal skills are highly regarded by some organizations, they are seldom taught or incorporated in training programs. Businesses teach their employees how to operate machines and how to use software, but not how to work with people. It is imperative that a training program on civility be

!@!%#!@!%#!@!%#!@!%#!@!%#!@!%#!@!%#!@!%#!@!%#!@!%#!@!%#!@!

Sprint Code of Conduct

A Code of Conduct reinforces the Sprint Quality Principle of "Respect for People" in meetings and in daily communication with others. You may use the Code of Conduct shown below or modify the Code to best suit your needs.

The Way We Run Our Business
Sprint Quality—Code of Conduct

- Respect Each Person
- Share Responsibility
- Question and Participate
- Attend All Meetings; Be on Time
- Listen Courteously
- Keep an Open Mind
- _____
- _____
- _____
- _____

conducted in the workplace before one will see results in that community.

As I've said previously, patterned niceness or spot etiquette training will not even make dents in the armor of incivility, much less eradicate the problem in the current climate. You have to teach an *approach* to life in general—and work life in particular—if you want respect to permeate your workplace. And you have to provide people with the support they will need to effect change. Once the decision has been made to implement a civility program, the necessary resources must be allocated for books, manuals, consultants, and workshops. Halfway measures are not going to solve your civility problem.

Further support can be provided in the form of coaching for individuals who may feel that they need additional help after a workshop or who desire lessons in other essential areas such as time and organizational management, listening skills, letter writing, or improved English skills. It has been my experience that after a general civility course, employees also start requesting advice on dining and other social skills they may never have been taught at home or in school. Self-improvement is contagious!

Additional Training Tools: Aids for Limiting Stress and Setting Expectations

In addition to materials specifically focusing on civility, a number of other training resources can help promote a climate of civility. One of the most valuable ways in which to encourage a more stress-free and civil atmosphere in the workplace is to provide tools that help work processes proceed amicably and communication go smoothly.

Two of the most critical areas where incivility can occur are those of meetings and problem solving—both of which are addressed by our exemplary friends at Sprint in the *Sprint Quality Handbook,* which is distributed to every employee in print form and posted on their intranet. Not only does this distribution get useful information into the hands of every employee, it also sets expectations that prevent the workplace from becoming a bazaar filled with hagglers and nurtures a corporate culture.

The section of the handbook on meetings covers preparing for a meeting, writing an agenda, brainstorming, arriving at an action plan, and taking minutes. It employs user-friendly acronyms such as PAL to help employees remember the three key points of planning a meeting: purpose, agenda, and limits. The fact that vote taking can be isolating is discussed, as well as consensus decision-making processes, with an emphasis on win-win situations. Sample forms for meeting observations and post-meeting checklists are also included. Teams and units interact better when they are given such tools to work with. Everyone knows what is expected and there is less frustration.

The section on problem solving describes various forms of solving problems and looks at such methods as having an open discussion or generating ideas silently. It covers statistical data (including the difference between quantitative and qualitative data) and walks readers through problem-solving steps, teaching the meaning of control charts and distributions in a bell curve—even how to benchmark and prioritize matrices. All the members of a team are on the same page with the help of an aid like this, and less time is wasted.

Notice that this material comes out of the *Sprint Quality Handbook*. Usually, organizations approach quality only from the narrow perspective of innovation, product development, service delivery, or profit. Rarely do they emphasize the holistic approach of enhancing the behavioral culture for all stakeholders in an organization. World-class performance among employees and others they interact with on a daily basis doesn't happen by chance.

My suggestion to all organizations is to come up with a similar handbook for your employees. If your resources are limited, produce a small, photocopied handout. It makes employees feel in control, gives them the know-how to produce, and is the best confidence builder around.

Prehire Screening and On-the-Job Performance Appraisal: Put Teeth in Your Civility Program

No civility policy will succeed if a civility component is not built into hiring practices and evaluation processes.

Prior to hiring a new employee, references should be checked out thoroughly with an eye toward detecting any patterns of incivility, such as aggressive tendencies or abusive behaviors. Not all organizations document such incidents and not everyone will be comfortable discussing them, but you have to inquire. Just asking if a former employer was ever aware of such an incident opens up the topic to discussion, with the possibility that more may be divulged.

During interviews, evaluate the fit of prospective employees and ask direct questions about people skills. You have to determine what their behavioral traits are and whether they are commensurate with the candidates' other skills. Don't be afraid to ask if the candidate has personally observed incivility or abuse in the workplace and how she responded. You might try an exercise in which you give an interviewee a rude e-mail to respond to and see how he reacts. Or ask a prospective employee how she would handle a workday that entailed both a tight report deadline and a mandatory unit meeting.

Sometimes, just initiating a discussion on manners can give you insight. If the individual laughs nervously or derides the topic, you know that you have a problem on your hands. Asking about how a former employer handled civility issues and listening carefully to the reply will provide a good indication of the candidate's attitude toward respectful behavior. If he raises his pinkie finger in mockery, show him the door (believe it or not, I have seen this happen!). If a prospective employee's cell phone rings during the interview, think twice before hiring her.

It is absolutely necessary that all employees understand that in evaluations the appraisal of their civility quotient will carry as much weight as the appraisal of other skills. It is to their distinct advantage to ensure that no infractions are registered with supervisors or the Human Resources department. At the conclusion of any organization-wide training program, provide employees with copies of the civility policy as included (or to be included) in the company handbook, as well as handouts that list civility-related appraisal criteria or the basic principles on which they will be evaluated. Expectations must be clearly communicated!

Of course, managers and supervisors must work with their staffs on these issues all year long and throughout the entire

!@!%#!@!%#!@!%#!@!%#!@!%#!@!%#!@!%#!@!%#!@!%#!@!%#!@!%#!@!%#!@!

Points to Include in Performance Appraisals

• Exhibits a generally cooperative attitude (does not mean that they always have to agree)

• Settles disputes and disagreements without rancor or shouting

• Listens generously

• Is punctual in daily attendance, office meetings, and handing in reports

• Shows consideration for others—does not treat people like children or disparage them and spread rumors

• Does not undermine the credibility of others

• Is not noisy, does not talk and/or scream across cubicle walls

• Demonstrates patience—does not rush everything

• Produces and delivers good, professional work

• Does not write nasty and demeaning e-mails, notes, etc.

• Takes pride in personal and office appearance

• Apologizes when wrong and does not blame others

• Uses appropriate language content

• Does not exclude people from meetings relevant to their work

• Contributes to a positive work environment and talks to everyone

• Produces quality work

• Uses a team approach when needed and nurtures cross-functional cooperation

• Is ethical

employment life cycle, not just at appraisal time. If someone is smoking in the bathroom in a nonsmoking building, leaving trash all over the lunchroom, chewing gum in a disruptive manner, or being gruff with customers, this behavior should be corrected immediately. The key is to watch closely for repetitious patterns versus a unique occurrence. We all have lapses.

However, if a violation of the expectations takes place that is part of consistently bad behavior, the incident(s) should be documented and filed in the employee's record. Often, coaching will be sufficient to ameliorate the situation—the offender might need to undergo sensitivity training or to work on skills in listening/responding or conflict resolution. These days, coaches find that many people have a problem with false high self-esteem, way beyond what their credentials and experience warrant, and a sense of extreme entitlement. Sometimes it is a matter of teaching a young professional that he has to pay his dues and that telling a supervisor to "f-k off" is not the solution!

If this approach doesn't work, then the severity of the infraction has to be taken into consideration and further action decided on. If all other interpersonal communication and civility training approaches fail, the last step is to provide an instigator with mandatory counseling.

Counseling: If All Else Fails

Incivility instigators are cunning and clever at avoiding public notice. Like other abusers and harassers, they often engage in their reprehensible conduct behind closed doors. At first it might be difficult to believe a negative report about a star performer. Do not punish the messenger or try to find excuses for the perpetrator. I was once told that an instigator's mother had died and therefore we had to excuse him. Not even a mother's death justifies the bullying and hurt that an instigator inflicts on his coworkers! And it is highly likely that the bad behavior was going on long before the death. The instigator got caught this time only because his guard was down for a split second!

If you highly value the technical skills of an employee with incivility problems that persist and want to keep the instigator on board and coaching has not helped, then your only remaining option is to mandate counseling; this is the last step in trying to help the individual. I am neither a psychologist nor a psychiatrist, so in my practice I refer people to professionals who can assist them. Typically, we find out that the individual has aggressive tendencies at home as well; often, there are childhood issues that were never resolved.

If you believe that people can straighten themselves out when provided with assistance and a second chance, counseling is the course of action to take. But be prepared for an extended process—and for the possibility of losing the good employee or the customer who was the target of the uncivil behavior. Personally, I would advise letting this type of worker go.

Transferring the instigator, which is only rearranging the problem, or promoting him away from the target (shocking, but not uncommon) simply creates problems for your business and for you in the long run. I must reiterate that incivility in the workplace not only affects those involved directly, it undermines the entire organization's effectiveness. The target of the bad behavior will tell other coworkers, who will tell customers, who will spread the bad news to the general public. Furthermore, the workplace environment becomes poisoned, morale diminishes, and commitment to the mission of the organization falters.

Incivility sets off a vicious cycle. It is the darker side of the work world that has not been talked about. Much like spousal abuse, child molestation, and sexual harassment in the United States 30 years ago, everyone knows workplace incivility exists, but most just ignore it.

Employee Attitude Surveys: Providing Feedback

Many organizations conduct mandatory annual Employee Attitude Surveys to measure satisfaction, identify areas for improvement, and keep management informed of employee concerns. An Employee Attitude Survey covers a broad spectrum of questions concerning management, the work environment, behavior, programs, merger issues, ergonomics, and overall corporate policy. It should not be limited to civility, but it is a good way to test how well your civility program fits in and is working. You can design an area of focus in the civility section, such as favoritism, yelling, or undermining others. (See page 51 to see how Shell devised their "Respect for People" response with the aid of an Employee Attitude Survey designed by International Survey Research.)

Employees should feel unconstrained and able to be forthright in completing these surveys. They should be allowed to fill out their forms at home, in a neutral environment, free from fear. Confidentiality should be stressed and comments may be entered anonymously, although the data is never to be used to personally attack others.

After the responses are processed at an independent site, results are distributed to group managers and every employee in a work group gets together to evaluate the results and develop an action plan that identifies who is responsible for each action item and the deadlines for completion. The highest level of reporting management becomes involved. If there have been incidents of incivility that employees consider harassing, these incidents tend to be revealed in this process; this is beneficial if an employee is afraid to report such instances directly to a supervisor or to Human Resources.

Secret Shopping: Feedback of Another Sort

With the rapid growth of large corporate chains and franchises in recent years, service has, at times, become impersonal, indifferent, or rude. Some of the more aware organizations have instituted another type of feedback mechanism to remedy incivility, in this case one designed to provide feedback about, rather than from, their employees. They hire moles who pose as customers to observe customer service and sales activities and evaluate whether corporate objectives are being carried out. This is called "secret shopping" or "mystery shopping."

About $425 million is spent in the United States on secret shopping. Businesses that use this type of feedback service include airlines, banks, health clubs, hotels, golf courses, public-transit systems, fast-food restaurants, and supermarket chains. Even some hospitals are beginning to use it! Secret shoppers observe the overall provision of service and note specifically the performance of employees with problematic track records. The evaluations generate results that are used to assess training needs, improve customer service, and reward the best performers. It is also a strategy to keep employees alert and on track, because they never know when a secret shopper will visit.

Some organizations hire top-quality people to perform this important task, but the role-playing, observational, and reporting skills of secret shoppers, unfortunately, vary widely—as does the effectiveness of the methodology.

Disseminating a Civility Campaign: Spread the Word

Now that management and the workforce are primed for the initiation of a civility program and all the needed policies, training programs, tools, and evaluation and compliance mechanisms are in place, it's time to start disseminating and reinforcing the message.

Pick and choose from the repertoire of communications mechanisms that follows to custom-design a campaign best suited to promoting civility in your workplace. Feel the pulse of your workers and determine what they will respond to best. Adapt the methods to fit your own particular needs; just do not do anything in a piecemeal fashion. Remember Jack Welch's advice to rally the organization.

Corporate Letterhead: Right There with the Logo

Correspondence on your organization's letterhead is often the first contact with customers, vendors, or prospective employees. Adding a civility message to your letterhead says right from the start not only who you are but what you believe in. It conveys a strong message about your corporate culture and sets a tone and expectations for future interactions. For example, at the bottom of the letterhead add one of these lines:

- Civility is good business. Thank you for choosing our polite company!

- We have trained our employees to be polite. Thank you for doing business with us.

- Rage is not our style. Civility is!

- Our employees will treat you nicely. Please reciprocate.

- Choose us as your business partner. We are never in a rage!

Marketing and Public Relations: Let Your Public Know What You Believe

Integrate the concept of civility in your strategic marketing and public relations plans and incorporate a civility message in every facet of your communications program. Position a civility statement prominently on all your brochures and printed materials, just as you do your mission statement or purpose. Create a civility message to work into your print and media advertising, such as:

- Civility is contagious—catch it—spread it!

- We respect you with courteous service. Please be nice to our employees.

- We promote a civil workplace for our employees and treat our customers with respect.

- At (name of your organization), we respect you!

Make up special slogans for billboards and marquees, such as:

- Shop with us—we treat you with good manners.

- Be our partner—we respect you!

- Do business with us—we will treat you right.

- Our employees practice civility. Our service is never enraged.

- Rage is out of style—manners are in!

Or even:

- Work here—our patience is a virtue.

Brochures/Newsletters/Magazines: Reinforce the Message Continually

Use brochures or handouts to further underscore key messages of the civility campaign internally, reminding your employees of the following:

- What the new policy is, how it will be enforced, and where to report incidents of incivility

- How workplace dissatisfaction is cultivated when incivility occurs (use statistics that demonstrate your point)

- How uncivil behavior leads to loss of productivity, diminished morale, and poor service

- How incivility can lead to depression, anxiety, and other mental health problems

- About your organization's desire that this workplace be as happy and stress-free as possible

If you produce an internally generated newsletter or magazine for employees and/or customers, incorporate articles on respect that delve further into some of these issues. If you employ a civility consultant, publish an interview with her; a recognized expert's views usually reinforce credibility and readers will pay close attention to the message. If you publish a wellness newsletter, include analytical pieces on the links between incivility and stress-related illnesses. Clip articles on respect and reprint them (with permission, of course); women's magazines and women's sections of newspapers are good sources of material, as are Human Resources and training journals.

Employees should not be bombarded with all this information at once, but piece by piece every six weeks or so. Incremental change is the only way to be effective.

Buttons and Bumper Stickers: Just Say "Yes" to Kindness!

We are a culture addicted by advertising to slogans and in the habit of proclaiming our beliefs and preferences on buttons and bumper stickers. Seize the opportunity and create buttons for all employees, including senior officers—this is very important—to wear. Adapt the same messages to bumper-sticker format and make them available to workers; this might even help with the road-rage problem as well as spread your organizational theme of goodwill!

Try messages such as:

- Respect matters.

- Be courteous.

- Slow down—be polite.

- Rage does not pay!

- Rage stinks!

- Civility counts!

Instruct your employees to engage clients and members of the general public in conversations about civility if they are asked what the button or the bumper sticker means. When employees start to talk about the civility policy and campaign in their own words, the message will get out. And, believe me, someone wearing a civility button at work is going to think twice before acting rudely!

Banners: Provoke Thought!

Create banners to display around the office, factory, store, or hallways that carry out the civility theme and get people thinking. They're hard to miss as you pass by and will implant the seed of an idea that will germinate through the rest of the walk. My friend Glenn Dromgoole, founder of Americans for More Civility (who can be reached at <www.morecivility.com>) suggested the following:

- Slow down and take the time to be more courteous.

- Spread a little civility—at work, smile more and complain less.

- Consider that you can be wrong at times.

- An attitude of gratitude is necessary because we were helped when we were helpless!

- How we use our time speaks volumes about our values.

- When people interrupt, shout, or throw chairs at each other on TV, turn it off.

- Pass it on—if you have been the recipient of a kind word or deed, do not let it stop there. Pass it on. Plant a seed.

- We won the lottery when we received an education that allowed us to read and think and earn a good living.

- The gift of hope—without hope, our lives have little purpose. With it, we can move mountains. Be helpful!

Posters: Potential Collectors' Items

Produce posters with civility messages to display in areas where employees congregate, such as cafeterias, lunchrooms, conference rooms, garages, reception areas, and in front of elevators. Here's where you can really be creative! People are attuned to clever advertising and public message posters, many of which become prized collectors' items long after their debut.
Here are some ideas:

- On a photo of the CEO proclaim, "I open doors for people." (Yes, it is funny and ironic, but it works wonders!)

- Show a picture of your building or lobby with the message, "Keep it clean!"

- Display a photo of a group of employees holding coffee mugs captioned, "We say 'Good morning.'"

- On a picture of a cheerful-looking employee say, "Simon says smile!" (I literally look for a Simon in every organization for this one—it is effective!)

- Show a secretary asking, "I write thank-you notes! Do you?"

These posters capture attention. They do generate laughter, but they work! Here are a few more possibilities:

- Group some of your most-masculine-looking workers in a shot captioned, "Refrain from vulgar language!"

- Display a granny-like employee who says, "Remember to RSVP—that means respond to e-mails, phone calls, and invitations."

- Picture a security officer with the slogan, "Respect the property of others."

- Snap the workplace "civility guru" and pair with the caption, "Etiquette honors commitment to quality and excellence—build your attitude" or "Manners inspire confidence for you to work with anyone!"

When you personalize the message, involve staff as models, and politely poke a little fun, the posters have more impact. They can be among your most effective media for conveying the civility message. People look for the next installment, read them, and talk about the themes! Just getting employees talking about the posters in their daily conversations is an achievement. They begin to internalize the ideas conveyed and eventually will start to apply them. Of course, you have to tailor the messages to address the particular problems most prevalent in your organization.

Telephones/E-mail/Computer Displays/Videos: Harness Technology

Don't forget one of the most obvious ways to get your theme across—incorporate a civility message in your standard telephone greeting. Much like adding a line or two to the corporate letterhead, this will set the tone with first-time callers and reinforce the culture with customers, vendors, and others. Train your receptionists to answer the phone in this manner, "Good morning, respect matters at (name of the organization). How may I help you?"

Organizations that disseminate e-mail messages to employees might periodically work in thoughts like:

- Make peace with someone you have had a disagreement with. Take him to lunch!

- Be nice to each other.

- Thought for the day: Work on your self-control.

Be careful not to overdo it though; employees typically receive too many e-mails these days.

Organizations with the means should consider incorporating civility messages (those suggested for banners would also work here) on computer monitor displays in the hallways or on the news tape in the elevator. I often visit companies who pay for CNN, but never think of substituting their own messages.

Another option for organizations that have the budgets to do so is producing training videotapes. This can be costly, however, and must be produced in a very professional manner to be effective. Scenarios of various faux pas, such as not standing up when a visitor enters your office, putting your hands behind your head, or leaning back in your chair with your feet on your desk, can be powerful training aids. Hiring actors to portray these behavioral situations in a way with which your employees can identify is the more viable option. Filming actual in-house behavior is difficult and has legal implications. If you want to feature actual staff, put together a script that demonstrates "Do's and Don'ts" and ask employees to volunteer to be actors. (But, once again, be sure that they are scripted, directed, and shot by professionals.)

Payroll Stuffers: What Better Means?

Some companies still mail paychecks to employees or distribute them in envelopes at the office. This is a wonderful opportunity to enclose a civility message along with a check. You certainly have the employees' attention! Here are a few suggestions:

Be Respectful

Use titles and pronounce names properly.
Treat others in the same way that you want to be treated.

Listen carefully when others speak—and respond nicely.

Be Fair

Be tolerant.
Listen to both and/or all sides. Then decide!
Say you are sorry when you are wrong.

Be Responsible

Respond to road rage by being exceptionally courteous.
Follow through on your projects and your promises.
Come to work on time and back from breaks promptly.

Be Nice

Report someone who is threatening to hurt someone else.
Keep the lunchroom clean and tidy.
Surprise someone at work with a thank-you note or small gift today!

Meetings and Special Events: Make Them Special Occasions

Sprinkle civility messages through your script for staff/weekly/strategy/marketing meetings. Relate the story about a particularly positive experience on a recent business trip. Describe the cultural phenomenon that you observed on a trip abroad and found outstanding. State in passing that you forgot to ask everyone to turn off their cell phones before the meeting and are pleased that so far no one has violated the rule anyway. Praise what you are currently observing as signs that people are showing new respect for their coworkers.

Make special events truly special and memorable in ways that reinforce civility. Try instituting a dress code or incorporating some ritual. On occasion, host a celebration, such as an English Tea Party, a French Champagne Reception, or an Argentine Tango Dance. Invite an etiquette expert to give a talk about dining etiquette during an organizational get-together or at a dinner retreat. These activities help create a climate conducive to implementing a civility program.

Use the Diversity Council: We Can Learn from One Another

One of my favorite ways to spread civility know-how is to hold programs through the diversity councils that most organizations now have in place. Ask foreign nationals working in your business to talk about some aspect of workplace respect in their native countries. A Japanese worker could relate how a code of conduct helps his compatriots work in overcrowded spaces and interrelate with a hierarchical structure. A person from an African country might discuss respect for the aged and their wisdom, detailing how African cultures tend to show deference to someone older in the workplace.

A person with a disability can give a presentation on etiquette for the disabled. Ask Irish-Americans or Latinos or Polish-Americans to talk about what we have lost compared to the civility quotient of their grandparents' generation.

Have an immigrant talk about some of the incidents that got her into trouble because of the different customs or manners in the United States. For example, I was taught that you should never stare a superior in the eyes during a job interview. One's head should be slightly bowed to demonstrate humility and that you are a good subordinate deferring to wisdom and experience. I finally realized, after doing some research, that I wasn't getting any job offers because U.S. Americans value eye contact. If you don't make eye contact, they think you are shifty and untrustworthy. I had to adjust fast!

Eliminating Profanity: Cussing Can Cost You!

One successful technique that I have used to curb workplace profanity is putting a "cuss jar" in every department to collect fines from folks who forget and swear. It's a lighthearted way to start enforcing the new policy. Vulgar words in any language (you can always tell when someone is swearing, even in another language!) should be fined. The executive office should have its own jar. Determine how much each profanity will cost and collect fines for charity.

I was at one client's holiday party during which the CEO divulged the results of his own unit's profanity elimination campaign. The penalty had been $1 per cussword and they had collected $250 during the year. Everyone applauded, and it drove home the point that the boss (who really did seem remorseful) is human as well.

Recognition and Reward: Positive Reinforcement

Many organizations have created ways to recognize and reward workers who exhibit good civility—an employee who was mentioned in the newspaper for doing a good public deed, or who displayed exceptional courtesy at a tough investor meeting, or who went out of the way to accommodate someone who was late in getting a project put together. A gift that is meaningful to the recipient is best; people just don't strive for the inscribed plaque or the commemorative paperweight. Of course, publicity in the house organ is always an incentive.

One of the most effective reward tools that I have come across is Sprint's On-the-Spot Award. The award—in the form of a handwritten thank-you note that coworkers send to one another or to vendors along with a special Sprint Values Excellence patch—is presented for special effort to achieve Sprint's goals and fulfill the company's vision.

I am enamored of this program for several reasons. First, because personal thank-you notes make a big difference, especially in this electronic age. Having a colleague take the time to write a note is one of the most significant ways that someone can be recognized in the workplace. It is especially effective that an individual employee can spontaneously send a thank-you without any committee or supervisory approval needed. The company provides each employee with note cards, envelopes, and patches. The embossed cards say, "Sprint Values Excellence on the Spot," and have a blank space inside for a handwritten message. What could be better than this approach to encourage appreciation of superb efforts among colleagues?

Most people find it difficult to offer verbal praise. Writing is easier and is a conversational icebreaker. The recipient can save the note for performance review purposes as well—her supervisor may have been too busy to notice that she went a bit above and beyond. Sometimes it is the little things, which usually go unrecognized, that matter.

Southwest Airlines, widely known for its customer-service orientation, follows a similar approach. It makes "Way to Go" cards available for colleagues to acknowledge and thank one another for extra effort. Southwest also has what they call the "Love Report" program (a clever language usage, for the airline's hub is Love Field in Dallas), through which a worker can send a letter of praise to the executive office about a fellow employee. The executive office then sends out a personal (not a form) letter recognizing the work of the recipient of the "Love Report." How is that for civility?

Reaching Out to Clients and Vendors: Civility Doesn't Stop at the Front Door

Any campaign to inculcate civility in the workplace must also be designed to reach clients, suppliers, vendors, and the general public with which the staff comes into contact. Remember, civility requires reciprocity to work and perpetuate itself. I read somewhere that we have become so obsessed with customer service that we have bred a rash of customer incivility! Customers have a responsibility to be polite as well.

If the people your staff deals with on a day-to-day basis are not informed and educated about your goals, your civility program will not be operating optimally. I advise businesses with large public clienteles—banks, hotels, health clubs, and retail stores—to incorporate many of the same techniques they use to disseminate civility to their workers. Send your customers a newsletter that features civility messages, or rotate theme-oriented poster displays in the lobby, or take out ads promoting your new concern with civility.

One large firm that supplies secretaries and paralegals to law firms noticed a big jump in business after I suggested that they promote their civility training program in promotional materials, guaranteeing that their temp workers were respectful in all competency skills. The firm even spelled out how they expected their temps to be treated in return.

Educating clients should be a major component of the process. Remember that putting a civility message in all marketing and public relations materials will help get the thought across to clients that *their* good behavior is also appreciated. We expect employees to be nice, but often we do little to let customers know that they are expected to behave as well. Employees in high customer contact positions get very discouraged by the behavior of people who seem to feel that if they are paying for a service, they are entitled to be rude. It helps greatly that these employees know the employer is concerned about their dignity.

Toward this end, for example, banks could sponsor free civility training seminars for customers, or give away etiquette lessons as part of their civility promotion. I advised one hotel to post its civility policy behind the reception desk, reminding guests checking in that *their* civil behavior was expected as well, and to include some civility suggestions in the hotel directory of services stocked in each room. I advised a high-end health club in Chicago to put posters around workout rooms, informing customers of their responsibilities as guests of the club.

Civility Council: Get Employees Involved

You may want to create a civility council to decide on ideas for implementing a civility program in your organization. A senior officer should chair the council to show commitment from top leadership. It should be comprised of one member from every department—not just Legal because of prospective lawsuits and Human Resources because of the performance issues involved.

Council members could be charged with forming subcommittees responsible for maintaining various public spaces and developing policy on what to do when things go wrong. They could form a liaison committee to work with the diversity council to implement programming ideas. Perhaps they could decide what the fine for cussing should be, where the posters promoting civility should be hung, or what rewards should recognize especially good behavior. The council might even be called on to create the overall civility policy for employees and to determine the consequences of breaking the rules. Getting employees involved with these decisions makes everyone take ownership of the program!

They might also select civility support representatives for every department; if there is a problem, a targeted employee would know who to report it to. These representatives would have to receive special training in listening skills, mediation, understanding the complex dynamics between instigator and target, and identifying their own limitations, as well as how to avoid burnout.

Personal Responsibility: Be Part of the Solution

Throughout this book, I have affirmed the need for personal responsibility in order for civility to occur. I want to reiterate that we cannot have organizational growth without all the individuals who make up the organization doing their part. Personal responsibility is paramount. My generation used to say that if you weren't part of the solution, you were part of the problem. Be part of the solution. Following are some ideas for reinforcing personal accountability that can be stressed in newsletters, on posters, or through any of the other communications mechanisms we have discussed.

Make an Honest Self-Appraisal

Make an honest assessment about how much you contribute to rudeness. It is not always the other person who is rude! Do you greet people in the morning? Say good night when you leave? Do you reply to e-mails and voice mail—or does the meeting planner have to call you repeatedly just to find out if you're going to attend the company outing? Do you come late to meetings and then insist on having everything repeated for you?

Have you become snappy lately? What might you have done to trigger an episode? If you were rude, did you go back later and apologize? If coworkers are constantly giving you the silent treatment, is it because they are jerks or because of some way in which you are behaving?

If you have problems in any of these areas, get some coaching to become a more responsible person. Your behavior is rude and unprofessional. If you just agree that civility is on the decline, but make no adjustments in your daily behavior to improve the situation, you are not playing your part.

Manage Anger and Stress

Examine possibilities that may work for you. Some people meditate. Others develop a fondness for a sport, either as a spectator or a player. Some people deliberately slow down their schedules, allowing only for one major job activity per day, or work in two or three leisure activities per week. Learn to plan your time, prioritize your calendar, and manage your life.

You do not have to always be busy to be successful. Despite the current affectation that if we do not put on an air of being overwhelmed, we are failures, running around like a chicken with its head cut off only demonstrates lack of control over your own life. For me, a great measure of leadership is to show people that you have time for them, even if you are busy.

Changing your ways of doing things at home will make your office life more livable. Decompress. Schedule less outside activities for your children and sit and talk as a family more often. Play cards or work on puzzles together. Garden as a family. Cook as a family and sit down together to eat and converse! Go for walks together. Run around less and spend less time and money on external amusements. Your children will appreciate your time in the long run and still get into good schools. I promise!

Deal with Rudeness

People are usually rude because they can be. It is that simple. There is very little rule setting at home or at work. And most of us are usually too timid to tell people that we do not want to be treated in a disrespectful manner.

If you make it clear in a polite way that you will not stand for rudeness, you will not be subjected to it. I advise employees who are treated badly to turn around and say, "I do not appreciate being treated in such a condescending manner. Please do not do that again." If someone interrupts you, say, "Please let me respond. I gave you a chance to make your point." If a coworker shouts expletives at you say, "I will talk to you when we are both calm." If you made an error and the supervisor starts yelling say, "I ac-knowledge that I have made a mistake, but I will not be yelled at. Please treat me as an adult."

When someone complains about a coworker being rude, do not make excuses for the perpetrator, such as "He has a dead-line." Think about ways in which you can help resolve the situa-tion before it festers and causes more stress in the work environment. Just saying "He is such a jerk. I hate him also." is counterproductive.

Be a Team Player

Lastly, try your best to go along with the civility program instead of always fighting cultural changes in your organization. Work with management toward consensus that will improve pro-ductivity, customer relations, and employee satisfaction and wellness. If you don't like the new rules, perhaps you should look for another firm where people swear, are disrespectful and stressed, but where you feel the "fit" is better.

As William Stephens notes in *Civility in an English Village* (Severn Books, 2000), if you value civility, you must have a mech-anism in place to help promote it. With regular communication about the civility program I have just outlined ways to imple-ment, and with systematic discussion about results as they are reported, employees will feel in the loop and will learn how to foster the goals. Once they start seeing the benefits, especially to themselves personally, you will have successfully launched the new culture.

I have included many examples of bad behavior in the work-place throughout this book, bad language and all. My purpose was to raise public awareness and make people realize that these are common problems and not isolated occurrences. Incivility in the workplace is not a new phenomenon, but one that has received little attention despite dramatically rising incidence in recent years. The evidence is glaring, and decision makers, including corporate counsel, need to confront it. After reading this book, I am certain you will agree that incivility is a gigantic problem detrimental to organizations in several ways.

Especially in this era of economic downturn, every business will have to find its competitive edge by creating an atmosphere of civility so that employees turn their full attention to customers and their needs, rather than bickering among themselves.

This book has dwelled on identifying problems and teaching solutions pertaining to the civility crisis that is fast draining employee energy, corporate productivity, and consumer good-will. Readers can and should consult the myriad of resources available on related issues not covered. I deliberately omitted details on dining etiquette and gift giving, both integral parts of the civility puzzle. I also chose not to expound on interview skills or formal writing and grammar. All are necessary in our day-to-day lives. However, so much has been written on these subjects and so very little on the burgeoning bad behavior crisis!

I should also mention my intentional omission of any discussion on the issue of sexual harassment, as well as other forms of discrimination that fall under the harassment umbrella, such as discrimination because of age, disability, ethnicity, gender, mar-ital status, national origin, race, religion, or sexual orientation. While I find any type of harassment reprehensible, these kinds of incivility are mainly illegal in the United States. And because they are against the law, they have already received considerable attention in the media and in the workplace, because most organizations are compliance-driven.

Only a handful of organizations have shown the wisdom to take behavioral policies beyond what is legally mandated. Business leaders have largely ignored the link between discrimination and less blatant acts of uncivil behavior. At the core of even the most seemingly innocuous incivility is the same fundamental lack of respect that characterizes more overt forms of harassment, but few corporate leaders have connected the dots.

I am not implying that the remaining body of incivilities should be criminalized. There is far too broad a spectrum to codify. And how would one gauge what types of bullying should be addressed by law and what actions are less threatening and better left out? Our European friends are struggling with this, and their laws inadequately cover the issues. Rather, I believe that we as organizations and as individuals need to learn how to do the right thing of our own volition. We need to have a change of heart on our own. I do not like the government always telling us how to behave; we ought to be personally responsible. The wise leader will recognize that it is cost-effective to be proactive in dealing with incivility and put a program in place before uncivil behavior escalates into a civil lawsuit, bad press, or violence.

I chose to address incivility in the *workplace* because logistically it can be tackled more effectively on an organizational level than individually. And let us remember that the workplace is everywhere, as the vignette at the beginning of Chapter 3 about trying to work in a cab demonstrates. The workplace does not stop at your own office door. If you live in a highrise, you depend daily on the competence and civil efforts of the workers in your building, and they rely on your consideration! If you own a single-family house, workers rebuild your roof, replace your boiler, and read your meter. When you are away on a vacation, you are eating and sleeping in other people's workplaces.

Where Do We Go from Here?

For starters, I think we have to examine whether this fast-paced life we live is what we really want to pursue. It is always easier to be rude when in a hurry. Civility takes a little extra time and effort. We have to ask ourselves if life is just about making money and working 24/7.

Perhaps what we need is a summit of major CEOs to consider a moratorium on our current way of doing things at work—lean and mean and thinking that humans can be as fast and robotic as machines. Maybe just as the wise called for restraint and disarmament during the Cold War, we now have to call for a rethinking of "business as usual" that is driving us to uncivil behavior. And changing the way we value speed over quality may help us slow down and realize that there are other possibilities; as we have observed, speed and quality are often incompatible.

Those of us who consult in the trenches certainly see the need for a more normal and livable pace to restore control and sanity to the lives of workers who are feeling completely stressed out and are striking back. We can see that a big cause of uncivil behavior in the workplace is the workplace itself. Unplugging workers and giving them more freedom to utilize a broader range of skills would help. For the past 15 years, organizations have neglected "soft" people skills, which I prefer to call emotional intelligence skills, in favor of the "hard" skills of technology. It is time for a better balance.

I would love to see some of the corporate stars band together to promote a more intelligent use of technology and to question the place of the gadgets and gizmos that keep us focused around the clock on our work, at the expense of our families, our interests, and our well-being. I am not a Luddite. I recognize that we need technology—but to help us, not to dominate us. Computer chips should not be more highly valued than people.

Furthermore, empowering employees to participate in making some of these decisions would lend a sense of autonomy, of being valued, and of doing something meaningful with one's work life.

I began this book with a historical analysis of how incivility came to be the problem it now is and would like to conclude with another brief historical perspective. After the fall of the Berlin Wall on November 9, 1989, we U.S. Americans were so euphoric about winning the Cold War that we turned away from the rest of the world and tuned out to little else but our own personal desires. We became obsessed with material extravagance and forgot about a national sense of purpose and about who we are as a people. We acted secure, selfish, and rudely indifferent even to one another's needs in our own communities and on our roads. Except for a small minority of religious groups and do-gooders, we as private citizens forgot about the blood-soaked conflicts still going on in many parts of the world and about the pain of others.

The terrorist attacks on our own soil on September 11, 2001, have reawakened us to the reality that we live in a global community, like it or not. Perhaps these tragic events will remind us as well that there is a purpose to our journey through life that is larger than self-gratification and that it begins with simple acts of civility and kindness to our fellow travelers.

Civility in the Workplace Quiz

This is a true/false quiz on "Civility in the Workplace." You get 2 points for a correct answer and 0 points for an incorrect answer. Please circle T or F for each question.

Score

T   F   1. Hostile, uncivil behavior at work can affect a
company's bottom line.   _____

T   F   2. The effectiveness of 22 percent of employees is
hampered by supervisors' uncivil behavior.   _____

T   F   3. Civility is a skill that cannot be measured and
evaluated.   _____

T   F   4. Stress is a major contributor to employees' uncivil
behavior.   _____

T   F   5. The problems caused by incivility often are reported
to management.   _____

T   F   6. Civility training can help diminish rumor spreading
and gossiping.   _____

T   F   7. Casual dress in the office can be a cause of employee
rudeness.   _____

T   F   8. In today's workplace environment, uncivil behavior
should be tolerated because it encourages
competition.   _____

T   F   9. Withholding praise from employees builds
              cohesiveness.   _____

T   F   10. Senior leaders should "walk the talk of civility."   _____

T   F   11. More than 30 percent of employees admit that
               they have yelled at coworkers.   _____

T   F   12. Accepting a gift from someone who would like
               to do business with you is wise.   _____

                                              Total: _____

Analysis:

20–24 points: You are a civility maven and/or a fast learner. You should play a lead role in ensuring civility in your Workplace.

16–18 points: You are beginning to see the light and ready to join the civility corps.

12–14 points: You should be first in line to learn more about civility and its benefits.

10 points or below: You should trade in your hammer for a horn and get on the civility bandwagon.

Answers:

1. True; 2. True; 3. False; 4. True; 5. False; 6. True; 7. True; 8. False; 9. False; 10. True; 11. True; 12. False

Sample Survey

INTRODUCTION

This survey offers XYZ Company employees an opportunity to express their views on a variety of issues related to the organization and their work experiences. The survey items were developed by International Survey Research (ISR), an independent consulting firm, together with XYZ Company employees.

YOUR OPINIONS ARE STRICTLY CONFIDENTIAL AND ANONYMOUS:

*   Completed questionnaires will be returned to ISR for tabulation.

*   ISR will report only statistical summaries of the results. No attempt will be made to identify individual respondents.

*   No one in XYZ Company will see any completed questionnaires.

The questionnaire is divided into two sections:

I. OPINION SECTION

    In this section, you are asked to express your views regarding a number of statements by marking the appropriate responses. There are, of course, no right or wrong answers. We simply ask for your opinion, based on your perceptions of the way XYZ Company, your business unit, and your functional area currently operate. In most cases, a "?" response option is provided for you to use if you cannot decide about a statement, if it does not apply to you, or if you have insufficient information to decide about the statement. In other cases, a "Don't Know" or "No Opinion" response option may be provided.

II. COMMENT SECTION

    This section provides you with an opportunity to write in any additional comments you think should be brought to the attention of XYZ Company management.

GENERAL INSTRUCTIONS

Because this survey is designed to be scored by machine, you must indicate your opinion on each statement by marking the appropriate box. Carefully observe these requirements:

*   Use a soft lead pencil.

*   Place a heavy "X" in the box.

*   Mark only one opinion for each statement. If you want to change an answer, erase completely and put an "X" in the correct box.

MARKING INSTRUCTIONS	
CORRECT	INCORRECT
☒	☑ ③ ▣

Multiple marks cannot be counted.

---

303 East Ohio Street
Chicago, IL 60611
(312) 828-9780
FAX: (312) 828-9742
www.isrsurveys.com

I. OPINION SECTION

The "?" response is provided for you to mark if you do not have enough information, or it does not apply to you.

	Disagree
MARKING INSTRUCTIONS	Tend to Disagree
CORRECT INCORRECT	?
☒ ☑ ③ ▣	Tend to Agree
	Agree

1. I have a very clear idea of my job responsibilities .... ① ② ③ ④ ⑤

2. Company management is interested in the well-being of employees .... ① ② ③ ④ ⑤

3. My supervisor does a good job of building teamwork .... ① ② ③ ④ ⑤

4. The people I work with usually get along well together .... ① ② ③ ④ ⑤

5. Management of this company supports diversity in the workplace (recognizing and respecting the value of human differences) .... ① ② ③ ④ ⑤

6. The information I need to do my job is readily available .... ① ② ③ ④ ⑤

7. I understand how my performance on the job is evaluated .... ① ② ③ ④ ⑤

8. The company makes adequate use of recognition and rewards other than money to encourage good performance.. ① ② ③ ④ ⑤

9. My work gives me a sense of personal accomplishment .... ① ② ③ ④ ⑤

10. In my opinion, this company is socially responsible in the community .... ① ② ③ ④ ⑤

11. Work is usually distributed fairly among employees in my department...................... ① ② ③ ④ ⑤

12. There is sufficient contact between management and employees in this organization .... ① ② ③ ④ ⑤

13. My supervisor seldom gives me recognition for work done well .... ① ② ③ ④ ⑤

14. Employees are treated with respect here, regardless of their job.............................. ① ② ③ ④ ⑤

15. My supervisor effectively works with people who are different from him- or herself (in gender, racial/ethnic background, lifestyle, etc.) .... ① ② ③ ④ ⑤

16. This organization does an excellent job of keeping employees informed about matters affecting us .... ① ② ③ ④ ⑤

17. Performance reviews are conducted on a regular and timely basis in my department .... ① ② ③ ④ ⑤

18. Compared with other people working here, I think I am paid fairly .... ① ② ③ ④ ⑤

Disagree
Tend to Disagree
?
Tend to Agree
Agree

19. In my experience, all employees are held to the same standards of ethical behavior .. ☐1 ☐2 ☐3 ☐4 ☐5

20. The amount of stress I experience on my job seriously reduces my effectiveness ...... ☐1 ☐2 ☐3 ☐4 ☐5

21. Management is generally respected by employees .... ☐1 ☐2 ☐3 ☐4 ☐5

22. This company operates with integrity in its: (Please answer *each* item.) ☐1 ☐2 ☐3 ☐4 ☐5

    a. Internal dealings (i.e., with employees) .... ☐1 ☐2 ☐3 ☐4 ☐5

    b. External dealings (with customers, suppliers, etc.) .... ☐1 ☐2 ☐3 ☐4 ☐5

23. This company makes hiring decisions based on the skills and experience of the applicant, regardless of age, gender, ethnic background, or disability .... ☐1 ☐2 ☐3 ☐4 ☐5

Very Dissatisfied
Dissatisfied
Neither Satisfied Nor Dissatisfied
Satisfied
Very Satisfied

24. Overall, how satisfied are you with your job? .... ☐1 ☐2 ☐3 ☐4 ☐5

II. COMMENT SECTION

Please print your comments in the space provided below. Your comments will be typed and reported anonymously. Please identify the subject of each comment by placing the appropriate category topic number from the list below in the box beside your comment. Use only one category topic number for each comment.

Please provide any comments you would like to make or any additional ideas you have for improving XYZ Company as a place to work.

1. Job Satisfaction	6. Customers
2. Total Compensation	7. Diversity
3. Career Development	8. Efficiency
4. Change	9. Health & Safety
5. Respect	10. Integrity/Ethics

THANK YOU FOR YOUR PARTICIPATION.

THIS IS THE END OF THE SURVEY. PLEASE DO NOT WRITE ON THIS PAGE.

Giovinella Gonthier brings extensive international experience and training skills to global companies. She has served as an ambassador to the United Nations in New York City and in Washington, D.C.

A sought-after trainer and speaker, Ambassador Gonthier has made numerous presentations before the UN, universities, business organizations, and international conventions throughout Africa, Asia, Central America, Europe, and the United States.

Ambassador Gonthier has a B.A. from Wheaton College in Massachusetts and an M.A. from Harvard University. In May 1985, she was the recipient of an honorary doctorate (LLD) degree, conferred by her alma mater Wheaton College for her record in public life. She is fluent in English, French, Creole, Spanish, and Swahili.

Currently, Ms. Gonthier is president of her own consulting company, Civility Associates in Chicago, specializing in civility in the workplace training, etiquette classes, and high-end corporate gifts. She has experience at all levels of civility and etiquette training and is knowledgeable about respect and civility as they relate to other cultures. Her professional background in education helps in teaching methods and needs evaluations, whether conducting workshops for adults or children. In the area of civility training, Ms. Gonthier has combined her diplomatic knowledge with her background in education for creative exercises.

Ambassador Gonthier can be reached at civilityassoc@hotmail.com.

O R D E R   F O R M

A. Workbooks

1. 10 workbooks without binders....................$350.00
   (A Teacher's Manual included)

2. Title Page in color for binder cover $4.00

3. Handling Charge $10.00

4. Shipping .... Extra

(The teacher's manual is available only with workbook orders. The workbooks and teacher's manual are not bound. Each page has three holes punched for a ring binder; binders not provided. All sales are final and materials are not returnable. The workbooks and teacher's manual are copyrighted and may not be reproduced in any manner.)

B. Buttons

1. Buttons are $1.00 each and sold in sets of 25 ....$25.00

2. Handling Charge $4.00

3. Shipping .... Extra

E-mail order inquiries to: civilityassoc@hotmail.com. Or fax orders to 312-655-8454. Mailing address for payment will be provided on completion of order.

Managers and HR Professionals—Take Action!

BUILD A REWARDING and productive work environment. Order *Rude Awakenings: Overcoming the Civility Crisis in the Workplace* in quantity to create a culture of civility among all of your employees. Contact Mindi Rowland in Special Sales at 800-621-9621, extension 4410, or by e-mail at rowland@dearborn.com.

Your company also can order this book with a customized cover featuring your name, logo, and message.

Dearborn™
Trade Publishing
A **Kaplan Professional** Company